TENDERNESS IS STRENGTH

By the same author

Learning to Feel—Feeling to Learn
It's Me and I'm Here!

Tenderness
Is Strength

FROM MACHISMO TO MANHOOD

by Harold C. Lyon, Jr.

with the editorial assistance of Gabriel Saul Heilig

HARPER & ROW, PUBLISHERS

NEW YORK, HAGERSTOWN

SAN FRANCISCO

LONDON

TENDERNESS IS STRENGTH: FROM MACHISMO TO MANHOOD. Copyright © 1977 by Harold C. Lyon, Jr. All rights reserved. Printed in the United States of America. No part of this book may be used or reproduced in any manner whatsoever without written permission except in the case of brief quotations embodied in critical articles and reviews. For information address Harper & Row, Publishers, Inc., 10 East 53rd Street, New York, N.Y. 10022. Published simultaneously in Canada by Fitzhenry & Whiteside Limited, Toronto.

FIRST EDITION

Designed by Sidney Feinberg

Library of Congress Cataloging in Publication Data
Lyon, Harold C
  Tenderness is strength.
  Includes index.
  1. Men—Psychology. 2. Tenderness (Psychology)
I. Title.
BF692.5.L96   152.4'2   76-26242
ISBN 0-06-012713-9

78 79 80 10 9 8 7 6 5 4 3 2 1

To my Father
a beautiful and warm human being
and a tender role model for a son

Acknowledgments

Special thanks go to Gabriel Heilig, my "brother," not only for his substantial contributions to this book in terms of prose and thorough editing, but for the inspiration to me from his unique willingness to share his tenderness and be a catalyst for mine.

There are many others who deserve acknowledgment and particularly Carl R. Rogers for his powerful influence as a tender role model for me personally and professionally; David N. Aspy for his strong support as a "militant humanist" and coach during a particularly painful period when the going was rough for me; Werner Erhard, founder of est, for the space he has helped create and open for me in my continuously transforming life since taking the est Training.

Thanks to Barbara Hider for her diligent energy typing the manuscript.

I want to acknowledge Virginia Hilu and Hal Grove, whose enthusiasm toward my manuscript in its earlier days and warmth toward me will always be remembered. This book on tenderness was the last of hundreds Virginia so ably edited during her twenty-two years at Harper & Row, until her untimely death in 1976.

And finally, my warm thanks to my wife, Eta, who has helped me to rediscover over and over that I am tender and tough, strong and weak, good and evil . . . and still have a long journey to travel on the rocky road to human liberation.

The opinions expressed herein (obviously) do not reflect the position or policy of any U.S. federal agency, and no official endorsement should be inferred (ridiculous as that may sound).

Contents

Foreword

by John Denver

Wherever I go in the world these days, I can see manifestations of personal and individual growth; a greater understanding of ourselves not only as human beings, but as men and women, parents and children, players and workers, blacks, whites, Indians, Christians, Communists—all the different elements that exist in the greater context called Humanity.

One of the most beautiful manifestations of this evolutionary process is the increased desire to communicate out of our own personal experiences, not just our observations of the world around us, or the knowledge passed on by previous generations, but to share ourselves with one another; to say, this is how it is for me and I want you to know, I need you to know. Certainly this is an accurate description of what is going on between men and women today.

Tenderness Is Strength is a clear and honest communication about men's lives and the place of tenderness in male psychology, directed toward the ultimate liberation of men and women. It is truly the most comprehensive and compelling statement of tenderness that I have ever read. This book is a testimony to the power of love and the beauty of tenderness as an aspect of maleness.

Hal Lyon, with whom I share the honor of serving on the National Advisory Board of est, is a not-so-unique man with a totally unique story to tell. This is simply his story. Born into a military family, he has served as a West Point cadet, a para-trooper, and a top federal official in government. He is now leading an international project to create Olympic Games of the Mind and Senses for gifted youth from all over the world. He has authored books on feelings and openness, on his own personal growth, and now this book on tenderness. In all of this, he has shown a real commitment towards sharing the truth of his own experience.

I am grateful to Hal for the assistance he has provided me in the discovery of my self. I am grateful to him for providing the same kind of opportunity for you.

Whether man or woman, partner or parent, young or old, come read—and remember—and realize once again who you are. *Tenderness Is Strength* is a book which makes it safer for all of us to be ourselves, and to share ourselves with one an-other.

August 1977

TENDERNESS IS STRENGTH

Introduction:
The Rainbow and the Laser

Something very exciting is "busy being born" in America today: a new sense of what it means to be a person—male *or* female. And with it, a new sense of what America as a nation can be. We are now living through a period of transition from various forms of chauvinism to a new, shared sense of humanity. This transition is occurring rapidly at the levels of both individual and national consciousness. We are doing more than changing slogans. We are actually expanding our understanding of who we are.

Much of the energy for this breakthrough now is bound up in the struggle to free both men and women from centuries of sex-role stereotyping. We are in a very real birth process, and the labor is often painful. This book is about part of that struggle and part of that birth. This book is about tenderness and strength in the lives of men.

Many men seem to suppose that they have little need to be concerned about tenderness—or that any connection between tenderness and strength even exists. Strength generally is thought of as a direct, manly quality, while tenderness is seen as a weaker, feminine trait—one that men have little reason to be curious or concerned about. Little boys are taught that tenderness is all right for nurses and mothers, but strength is needed by cowboys, soldiers, and policemen.

Unfortunately, as we will see, this simplistic child's view is carried over into our adult lives. Men grow up assuming that women are weak and "emotional." Yet Ashley Montagu and many other researchers have found that it is women who possess greater stamina and endurance. And as for being "emotional," as someone once put it, "women are petty about petty things, and serious about serious things—while with men it is just the reverse."

However, my purpose in writing this book is not to score points for either side in the sexual cold war which recently has frozen relations between many men and women in our country. My purpose is to explore the meaning and importance of tenderness, and to examine how it is related to strength.

Recently a great deal has been written about women's liberation, and more recently about men's liberation. I have not written this book specifically about either one, although I support both. As a man, I recognize that women's liberation is necessary as one of the means by which men's psycho-social evolution will be secured and enhanced. Likewise, I see much value in men's liberation as a way of freeing myself and other males from the deadening stereotyped roles and behaviors that have too often and too easily claimed too many men and women—and children. However, I have not focused on those aspects of our biology and consciousness that are simply male or female.

I see both men's and women's liberation as steps on the path to a richer and more unified awareness. Between men's and women's liberation, and surrounding them both, lies a vast unexplored and exciting area of conscious experience. Sexual awareness is only part of a larger and much more comprehensive *human* awareness. It is that hidden area on the spectrum of consciousness which is not specifically male or female, but specifically human, that I have sought to bring forward in this book. It is our humanity we seek to liberate here, not our maleness or our femaleness. The human heart has no gender.

The sexes are not really "opposite." In my mind, and in this book, I regard the two sexes as being *complementary* rather than opposite. Psychologists and philosophers ranging from those of ancient China and India to Carl Jung have taught that male and female elements exist in the makeup of every human being. None of us is entirely male or entirely female. All of us are partly each. And we are all complete. It is our understanding which is incomplete, not ourselves.

For me, this book is both an end and a beginning. It marks an important transition in my own life and in my understanding of what my life is all about. One long chapter in my life is drawing to a close, and another is opening, one which I hope will be more fulfilling.

What is ending in my life is my subservience to the kind of self-image and self-presentation that is summed up by the word "machismo." What is in the process of being born is my manhood.

The growth process from machismo to manhood has not been easy or immediate. And it is not over, by any means. But it has begun. And it has already moved my life in directions that are totally unexpected and truly exciting. My work here has been a key part of that process for me.

The purpose behind this book, however, is not to share my own personal history. It is, instead, to reflect upon my search for my true selfhood and to share whatever wisdom my experience has given me, so that others can see past my own errors and make use of what these errors have taught me. I have had many

lessons. Some have been painful, and many have been exquisitely beautiful. I am excited to share what I have begun to
learn, not only because it is happening within me, but because
I suspect that what has begun to happen within me has also
been happening in the lives of many people. I do not see myself
or my story as an isolated phenomenon but as part of a much
larger pattern that now is shaping itself in the lives of many men
and women across America.

In this book I have attempted to explore the source of an
understanding and a consciousness which can liberate not just
part of our aliveness—the male or female part—but *all* of what
we are.

At times this has led me to discuss ideas which are philosoph-
ical, controversial, and abstract. Wherever I have done so, I
have done my best to keep my discussion plain and direct. My
intention is to communicate with you.

Attempting this, I have not hesitated to delve at times into
areas of human experience, and particularly sexual experience,
which I feel to be significant on the path to a deeper understanding of who we are, and can be. At times these discussions
are very frank and personal. My intention in these instances has
not been to shock anyone but simply to discuss openly and
candidly aspects of human experience which I know can be
difficult as well as rewarding. I make no pretense of having
"answered" all of the many vital questions about these areas of
experience. I am not a saint, as my friends and family know full
well. I have simply done the best I can, sharing what I feel I
have learned from my own life experience, reflecting upon my
past, and imagining what may lie ahead.

But how *can* tenderness and strength be related? They
seem like such polar opposites. (However, so do men and
women; and no one would argue seriously that men and women
are not related.) Still, the question remains, if only because we
have ignored it for so long.

I have invited a very close friend, Gabriel Heilig, to collabo-
rate in preparing some of the material for this book. He has
suggested a way of looking at this question which illustrates
very clearly the intimate and powerful relationship between
tenderness and strength.

"Think of light," he says.

"Light is the most basic energy of our lives here on earth.
Without it, we would perish.

"Yet light is very subtle. It is the softest, most intangible sort
of energy. It is so present that we tend to take it completely for
granted. Its power is not always obvious, it is so enveloping.

"Now think of the sunset, or a rainbow, or a candle, or the
first light of dawn. All of these images of light evoke immediate
responses of tenderness. They are, in fact, classic images of
romance and serenity. We do not ask why we respond to them.
We respond without asking. They are part of our intuitive
knowledge of life.

"So, on the one hand, light is the stuff of rainbows, dawns,
and midnight trysts by candlelight. And on the other hand, it
is the overpowering suddenness of lightning and the penetrating, unbreakable beam of the laser."

Gabe's illustration is useful, for it points out that two apparently opposite qualities can be manifestations of the same energy. As we look more closely at tenderness and strength, I
think we will find that they, too, are intimately related in ways
we had not suspected. And when we begin to look beyond the
artificial distinctions which have been drawn around them, I
think we will discover that there is far more to these "simple
opposites" of tenderness and strength than we first supposed.
We may find that they mirror each other, and ourselves, in
some fascinating and revealing ways. And we may also discover that, as men, we are not forever chained to a caricature
portrayal of one cartoon quality over and over and over again.
For many men that discovery may be a little frightening at

first, but it also can be enormously releasing and creative.

That discovery is the purpose of this book.

The basic teaching of every true master, every saint, and every religion of humankind is that we are all One. When we have felt the truth of this in our own hearts—and have learned to experience and express its truth in our daily lives—then we will know that, in the deepest sense, we are all lovers.

If you feel that this message is close to the tone of your own heart, I invite you to share in this book.

1 Liberating the Woman in Every Man, the Man in Every Woman

Nothing is so strong as gentleness.
Nothing so gentle as real strength.

ST. FRANCIS

During the past few years there has been such a furor over women's liberation and, now, men's liberation, that many men and women have forgotten that all of us are *human*, first and foremost. Many women have become so caught up in their struggle for equal rights that they regard men as "the enemy." Men, hurt and confused by the new feminist attitudes, have begun to set up a liberation movement of their own. This sudden polarization of views between the sexes is most likely a passing moment in the overall history of the consciousness movement, a regrouping before the next evolutionary step. It is, after all, a little difficult for a society to remain permanently fixed in a situation in which both men and women regard each other with mistrust and suspicion. Children have to be born and raised by parents, not by liberationist cadres. Male and female homosexuality may be a choice for some, but it is hardly the answer for everyone.

Nevertheless, the feminist movement has served as a very

powerful stimulus for consciousness raising by both women and men. Prevailing attitudes and practices in work, family life, sexual relations, and self-identity have all come under the scrutiny of outraged women, who have only recently become vocal about their own condition. Like blacks and the many immigrant groups who have settled here, American women are finally staking their full claim to the bounties of American life. This can only be to the good. It strengthens the society, clears the air, and gets rid of old and outworn biases. Space is created for new relationships—between men and women and among groups of women.

Now men are beginning to connect with one another also, to create men's support groups just as women have done over the past ten years. Men need this kind of brotherly support very much. The poses and postures men have to assume in the business world and in their social, sexual, and family lives can take a murderous toll. And they do. The life spans of American men continue to drop, not because of raging epidemics, but because of the cumulative stresses of contemporary life. And the men who are the most vulnerable are those who seem, outwardly, to be the most successful.

Their blood pressure keeps increasing along with their salaries. For, despite temporary tactical victories in the bureaucracies of business or of government, there is never much certainty in these paper worlds. The survival quality needed there is not assertiveness but the ability to sit on the fence and appear "thoughtful," while testing the winds to see which way a thoughtful man ought to face. As the late sociologist C. Wright Mills once noted, "A bureaucracy is no testing field for heroes." Instead, as we now know, it is the breeding ground for ulcers and mental strain, absent fathers and multiple divorce.

It is no wonder these men seek "liberation" in mistresses and martinis, sports cars and sports. But objects do not replace feelings, and kicks are no substitute for stability. So now at long last men are beginning to seek one another out to create a common ground upon which to rebuild their confidence and to express their softer emotions, which have been suppressed and starved during years of dissembling and self-avoidance.

It is not a moment too soon. Men have become isolated inside the barren barricades of machismo, afraid to let anyone in and afraid to let themselves out. They live in constant fear that someone will see, behind the loud posturing, a lonely person locked inside himself. The rage and helpless feelings which result are hard to share. To those who can read it, the language of machismo is a distinct plea for someone to finally break through the rigid postures in which so many men have become trapped.

As W. H. Auden put it once in a poem, "Each in the cell of himself is almost convinced of his freedom." But the macho will not let go of his pose, cannot relax his stance. It is what he longs to do, and it is what he most fears doing. He must triumph. He will not share. He trusts no one—least of all himself.

This distortion of maleness into machismo caricatures masculinity. It alienates men from their own feelings and makes maleness into a narrow and confining set of qualities—monopolized, of course, by men. It also creates an unnecessary and artificial gulf between men and women.

By the logic of machismo, "Men are men, and women are women." This sounds very obvious and clear-cut, yet the facts of human psychology and sexuality suggest otherwise.

The Yin and Yang of It

Studies now being done on maleness and femaleness support the picture drawn thousands of years ago in Asia. Men are not all male. Women are not all female. Each is partly both. The

American poet Robert Bly has put it very well in a recent interview:

The Taoist Chinese avoided the . . . words "male" and "female" . . . They took a step back into their psyches and invented two consciousnesses, the red and the green. The red, or *yang*, consciousness involves certain energies, no matter who feels them.*

The red, or yang, consciousness is the driving, initiating, rational energy—the one we usually think of as "male." But it is not confined to men. Women also possess ample yang potential. And likewise the green, or yin, consciousness—complementary, yielding, dark, and mystery-filled—is what we often think of as "female." Yet it is not limited to women. Inventors, poets, scientists, and mystics are all touched with this green, yin, consciousness. Through the continual interaction and interpenetration of the red and the green, the yang and the yin, the "male" and the "female," this world is continually re-created. Maleness alone does not do it. Nor does femaleness alone do it. It is the constant shifting advance and retreat of light and dark, reason and unreason, the known and the unknown, which together give the world its taste, its clarity, and its attractiveness to us.

None of us is entirely "male" or entirely "female." We are all a mixture of these energies, which exist in the world naturally just as they exist in us. We are not always expanding (yin) or always contracting (yang). There are times for movement in each direction. The natural process of living involves contact and then withdrawal.

One cannot keep on eating and eating; time must be allowed for repose and digestion. Even lions sleep.

In this respect, we can begin to see that to be a "man" involves more than being totally "male." One must be able to go beyond an isolated definition to embrace the full spectrum

*"Interview with Robert Bly," *East West Journal,* August 1976.

of one's psychic potential, a spectrum which includes "female" aspects. A key element of Carl Jung's psychology was his concept of the "shadow self," the anima, or "female," element in men and the animus, or "male," element in women. This "shadow self" is the secret stranger who always lives inside us. For men she is the woman of our dreams—literally. For women he is the longed-for hero, the epitome of what the woman feels within her to be male. These feelings are not fantasies, although they are often expressed in dreams and fleeting thoughts. They represent the hidden bonds uniting men and women.

The recent externalization of these qualities through the men's and women's liberation movements is a very healthy development, and one that gives added meaning to the wise and pungent remark made by William Sloane Coffin, that "the woman who most needs liberating in this country is the woman in every man, and the man who most needs liberating is the man in every woman."

When we can liberate *these* men and *these* women, then at last we will be fully and freely human.

Men's Liberation As a Means to Women's Liberation

This book is a statement in behalf of men's liberation. Without men's liberation, the process of women's liberation may be interminably long and possibly tragic.

The best thing that could happen to women's liberation would be men's liberation. The worst thing that might happen to women's liberation would be that women would toughen themselves up in order to better compete in "a man's world," giving up their inherent tenderness in the process. It is a tragedy for some women who in the process of liberating themselves are looking on the competitive macho male as a role model.

By men's liberation I mean freeing ourselves as men from

the tough macho image society conditions us to live up to, and giving ourselves permission to allow the tenderness which is hidden within us all to surface. In the last few years, I have begun to discover that the toughness that I developed as a protective shell in order to survive in society's hostile environment is not really my strength, as I thought it to be. Rather, it is my *tenderness* that leads me to strength. Toughness is not strength. Tenderness is not weakness.

Now, I'm not advocating that males become meek, turning away at the first sign of conflict. Neither am I suggesting that we should give up our ability to be tough (strong) when we need to protect ourselves in appropriate circumstances. From my early years in West Point, and as a paratrooper and Ranger Army officer, I needed a tough veneer to survive the rigors of living. So have many men in many other fields. Nor am I advocating total egalitarianism or indiscriminate interchangeability of roles between men and women. The yin and yang of physical and emotional differences between the sexes, if not the intellectual or spiritual ones, are differences which provide much of our joy and pleasure. However, when toughness becomes a way of life for men, as it often does in the corporate world, in the military, in government, in politics, and in many other walks of life, we tend to disown our tenderness—particularly when it is so often ridiculed, put down, or otherwise devalued in this competitive dog-eat-dog society. The rare and beautiful man is the one whose strength shines through his tenderness.

2 Toughness Is Not Strength

The simplest and most common words are often the most difficult to define. "Love." What is love? Thousands of books are written about it; no one ever exhausts the subject. "Strength" and "tenderness" are also qualities that are difficult to define. We think we know what they mean, until we have to pin them down precisely. I think that one of the reasons for this difficulty with defining these qualities, as with love, is that they are primarily inner qualities. We experience them inside ourselves, and then we must use words to seek agreement with others about what these internal experiences have meant to us. No one has much difficulty defining what a policeman is or what a Cadillac is; these are external. But what really *is* strength, and what *is* tenderness—and how are they related? These are questions this book seeks to answer.

One of the reasons inner qualities are so difficult to communicate about with any precision is that we live in a society in which so many of us gauge ourselves and others by the outward aspects of our lives.

Sociologists such as Max Weber and David Riesman have

pointed this out in their discussions on "conspicuous consumption" and "other-directedness." For many of us, "being rich" means owning a lot of objects with which we can show off; "being healthy" means having a dark suntan that everyone can see; "being happy" means laughing a lot at a party and giving the pretense of being happy. We often trade these outward symbols of "health" and "happiness" with others as though they were currency. Joe wants to go out with Suzanne, who has a nice suntan and looks good in a bikini. And Suzanne wants to go out with Joe because he has a Corvette convertible and everyone will be able to see how sharp she looks.

But do these people really know what their lives are all about? And are they willing to let anyone else know? Or are they too afraid to stop their mutual charade and take a look at what really is there behind the pantomime of pleasure?

Strength and tenderness are *inner* qualities. Our country's 193,000 fully equipped Marines don't make *me* as an individual any stronger. Saying "I love you" externally seventy-nine times a day to my wife doesn't make me any more loving to her. Saying it once from within, with feeling, does.

All too often we mistake the *symbols* of these inner qualities for the qualities themselves. We see someone with a muscular physique and we think, He must be strong. The fact is, he has a lot of muscles. How he uses them may be an entirely different matter. And how secure he feels about himself as a man may be still more removed from how he first appears to be.

In talking with physically beautiful women, I am amazed at how often they are genuinely unhappy, although they are the envy of most other women and the object of attention of so many men. "Object of attention" is part of the problem. You often hear attractive women say that they want to be loved and respected not just for their outer beauty, which they feel often gets in their way, but for their inner qualities as well—their

ideas, their emotional or spiritual aspects, which are less apparent than their surface qualities, and which it takes time to discover. The entire billion-dollar cosmetic industry exists because
of our emphasis on outer beauty, when it is inner beauty that
really counts if one wants more than a surface relationship or
"object" to show off. These women may be tempted to use their
own surface beauty to get what they want, which often leads to
more complexity in their lives.

Like the beauty of an outwardly stunning woman, the
strength of an overdeveloped, muscle-bound male is not free;
in fact, it is frozen in the hardness of his imprisoning "build."
The word is correct; such a body is *built*. It is not grown. And
it does not flow easily. The muscles get in the way and they
actually prevent the person inside them from expressing his
energy freely. They do not make him stronger. They use up his
strength. Unfortunately, strength is all too often thought of in
these terms. A "strong" man is *considered* to be one whose
voice is loud and sharp, whose muscles are hard, and whose
whole manner is tough. We all have known such "tough" men
in all walks of life. At times I have been such a person myself.

Training for Chauvinism

My training for male chauvinism took a dramatic and early
turn to the tougher side at age five. My father, a career Army
officer, left for World War II, leaving his little overachiever as
"man of the house," a responsibility which I took far more
seriously than he probably intended. I have a vivid recollection
of being with my mother as my father was boarding a train in
Cambridge, Massachusetts, in 1941. My mother was trying to
hold back her tears, and I was frightened as my father, without
malice or forethought, said to me, "You take care of your
mother and be good and I'll hurry home. You're man of the

house now." I'm five years old and suddenly I'm "man of the house"!

"You be good and I'll hurry home." That stuck in my mind. I tried so hard to "be good," to be a grown-up man of the house! And yet he didn't come home for three and a half years. I kept trying, thinking he didn't come home because I wasn't a good enough boy. I tried harder and became harder. When I'd get into fights at school (which seemed almost every day), instead of coming home with tears and bloody nose and crying in my mother's arms, I'd clean myself up and keep my pain, fear, and loneliness deep within myself so as not to burden her. If only I had shared with her and let her share with me the deep feelings of loneliness which were tearing me up inside, perhaps this would have built a bridge across which we could have shared our pain, which I'm sure was as intense for her as it was for me. (I realize as I write this that I'm once again putting man-sized expectations on myself as a five-year-old child. My mother might well have done some bridge building herself in this regard. We are often so hard on ourselves!)

In wanting so badly to take care of my mother, I literally grew up and became a man in many ways at age five. Instead of playing leapfrog, I leapfrogged over the carefree times of childhood, missing much of the playful tenderness that little-boyhood should be. This required me to "steel" myself, to harden and toughen up to survive in the world of adults. I put aside the toys of a child and became "a man."

I began to climb the ladders of achievement to get the re-wards that parents, teachers, bosses, and society hold up for the competitors in the arenas of life. I competed to get into West Point, the "toughest" place to get into and the most valued among the circle of military families in which I grew up. I finally won an appointment to West Point and then proceeded to climb through four years of what could accurately be labeled an excellent academic education (a broad academic program with small classes of fifteen students where we were graded almost every day). We cadets used to say, "It's a forty-thousand-dollar education—crammed down your throat nickel by nickel!"

At the same time, the West Point experience was the most efficient deconditioning of emotions and feelings that could possibly be contrived. "Public display of affection" was a punishable offense. I once received fifteen punishment hours for this offense—generally paid off by walking at attention with full uniform and rifle for fifteen hours or by sitting fifteen hours in confinement—when I was caught kissing my date goodbye after a football game. "You can't display emotion around here!" was a frequent threat made by upperclassmen to plebes (freshmen) who had not yet "learned" to bury their anger, fear, or joy. "Wipe that smile off your face, Dumb Smack!" was an often repeated negative reinforcement to those who couldn't help but show their amusement at the ridiculousness which often surrounded them.

The reason some West Pointers still have a sense of humor is that holding on to it became their main source of survival. Tears were unheard of.

I recall one young plebe who somehow made it through a tough "beast barracks" (the first summer for a cadet, equivalent to Marine boot camp). His father, a successful career Army officer, had forced his son to go to West Point "to make a man of him," not an uncommon situation. When shouted at by several loud-voiced upperclassmen for not being able to recite by memory "important" information such as "The Definition of Leather," he would invariably break down in tears. Plebes with any emotion and tenderness still operating in them always attracted the more sadistic upperclassmen. Tears were a sign of great weakness. "Tears are for girls!" I recall with considerable shame and chagrin how we systematically ran him out of the

Corps of Cadets using, of course, the official means of writing reports on his unsuitability as a potential officer with over- and undertones concerning the masculinity and possible homosexuality of a cadet who cried or could not control his emotions.

West Point is not alone in this. Many fraternities in institutions of higher education can be as bad, if not worse. At least West Point is frankly open about its chauvinism, and in some ways this is less frightening than the clandestine chauvinism of other institutions. West Point does have a point when it states that it is preparing officers to lead men in combat, where display of emotions could cause one to falter and fail to see the mission as being above all—and, often, above the lives of men. The military trains its men to guide their emotions into "acceptable" channels—patriotic feelings, camaraderie, and bayonet training.

I excelled in this red, white, and blue school of callousness and went on to do graduate work in toughness by becoming a paratrooper, a Ranger, and a counterguerrilla warfare instructor in the 101st Airborne Division. I spent seven years in the military, overdeveloping "that determination that will not be denied—otherwise known as 'guts.' "*

I cannot remember during those years ever considering or even suspecting or wishing that there might be a tender aspect to me. My toughness was my strength, or so I thought, and tenderness was a weakness in that environment. I was efficient and disciplined in my striving to achieve. I can recall thinking clearly what a waste of time it was having to stand in military formation four times a day (reveille, breakfast, lunch, and dinner; we marched to meals, church, and other functions of the day) seven days a week. My response was to use all that time to achieve more, by deciding to memorize mathematical con-

*Colonel John S. Roosma, member of the National Basketball Hall of Fame.

structs, formulas, and tables, which I did in my determination to be a better cadet and Army officer. I never stopped to realize that I was a unique human being just the way I was.

My dependence on time and my watch was far greater than I realized. It was not until sixteen years later that I was to realize how dependent I was on time.

I recall when I first went to bed with my wife, Eta, her being concerned that I had gotten into bed with my watch on. In my naiveté I thought she was concerned that I might break my watch. I told her that I had been wearing my watch to bed all my life and hadn't broken it yet. She replied that she wasn't worried that my watch would break. Doubly naive, I thought she was worried that it might scratch her, and I took it off, only to learn from her later that she was referring to the fact that melting together with someone you love is a timeless act. We unhook ourselves from time (and my watch) when we climb into our nest. There is no such thing as efficiency in good loving and the many other feelings, emotions, and delights I had been missing so much of.

My background with West Point and the military may seem like an exceptional case, and in some ways it is. But that's my point. If someone with my rather severe background can find the strength in his tenderness, then there is hope for all of us.

Moving Toward Inner Approval

I'm convinced that I climbed all the ladders of achievement that I could find primarily to earn the approval of others. I sought external approval rather than my own inner approval. Such is the case with many overachievers.

The approval we earn is not a "bad" thing. It does enable us to accomplish useful things and to gain a measure of material reward and satisfaction, and often to make significant contribu-

tions to society. But the driven nature of such *over*achieving is
the pathology of the overachiever. Just as a junkie seeks one fix
after another, we seek one achievement after another. Yet none
of them really satisfies us. Bigger and bigger doses of recogni-
tion are needed to feed the ravenous appetite of the driven
overachiever. What we really seek is more love and approval—
more of the holding, touching, and stroking we hungered for as
children. So being held by teachers, bosses, institutions, and
society becomes a substitute for being held by our parents.

Inevitably, then, I became an overachiever who displayed,
not my own hidden feelings of inadequacy, frustration, and
anger, but rather a compulsive need to master everything in an
effort to prove my worthiness to others. This was self-*image*
-actualizing, rather than *self*-actualizing—and they are quite
different.

Now, the traits I displayed are often widely admired. Parents, society, the military, the establishment, all value the
overachiever very highly. And he most likely will be rewarded
with status, promotion, material satisfaction, honors, and other
external rewards. For many years I never really believed there
were other important things!

But the rewards of environmental support for overachieving are not like the freeing support which comes from within
—rewards that I am now savoring more often. I'm in the sometimes painful, sometimes joyful, transition of beginning to get
my major satisfactions from within myself instead of from everyone else. I'm still something of an achiever, which isn't bad,
and probably I always will be to a degree, but more and more
I find the things I am achieving are things I really enjoy—things
that give me good feelings and approval from within, regardless
of what comes from outside. It's really a kind of falling in love
with my own inner self, not the all too familiar ego trip, which
is just the opposite of really loving yourself. The ego trip is a
mask to cover feelings of inadequacy.

I suspect that's how many of us become overachievers. If we're fairly bright or talented, we climb all the ladders to get the rewards held up by society, rather than reaching for the rewards from within ourselves.

But when we finally discover that we can get our rewards from within, it frees us in a new way. It's a freeing from being dependent on everyone else. It's growing from environmental support to self-support. This is what maturity is about—leaving the support of the environment and creating most of our approval from within ourselves.

People who get enough love and support early enough often develop their own inner approval systems earlier than those of us who have not been so fortunate.

My thirteen-year-old stepson, John, was nursed by his mother for four years. He's one of the few children I have ever known who has received that much holding and touching; and after seeing him, I'm convinced that there is no substitute for being held at the warmth and softness of the breast. And even he didn't get enough. No one does. However, John, a gifted child, is not constantly driven to achieve to earn the approval of others. He achieves for his own inner approval those skills he wishes to master. He does not go wanting for love and tenderness, waiting in vain for it somehow to come to him. He goes out and seeks it and gets a hug whenever he wants it. Tenderness comes naturally to him, it seems. I hope this will continue for him, in spite of schools and society.

I believe that in those earliest years the investment of touching is crucial. Though some radical feminist groups are anti-nursing advocates, they should realize they can help the human liberation movement far more by keeping their male and female babies at the breast, transmitting tenderness to them, than they can by feeding them with plastic bottles. Children nurtured at the breast will require far less "liberating" and will be

far more tender than those who haven't experienced this ultimate form of basic tenderness.

Growth Through Crisis

How does one find his or her tenderness in a competitive
society where we are constantly being rewarded for being
tough? How did my own life take a turn toward the tender
when I was so frequently rewarded for being tougher?

It was certainly not because of the "excellent academic curriculum" of West Point or the theoretical background given me
in my graduate academic courses. In fact, most of my academic
work was totally irrelevant to what I now value most in life. It
is easy to conclude that most academic work is a waste of
money, time, and energy when it is supposed to prepare us for
life and yet turns out not to contribute much that seems genuinely useful. The extracurricular activities and work on relationships with others are the saving grace of campus life. The things
I value most in life—openness, honesty, marching to my own
drumbeat, growing from environmental support to self-support, being centered enough to earn my approval from within
instead of being a slave to everyone else's "shoulds," love, tenderness, sensitivity, genuineness, the uniqueness of myself and
others, creativity, spontaneity, space to reflect and be me—
were gained in *spite* of, rather than because of, my formal
schooling. I never had a book assigned in my academic work
which contributed to these values. I have since found some
books—*after* gaining these values, rather than before—that do
lay out beautiful theoretical backgrounds for the things I now
value in life, none of which were ever assigned to me in class.

My growing to value those things occurred *after* the theoretical background had been imparted in academia, through
personal experiences, crises, and the painful, joyful process of
inner exploration through therapy.

It was the crises in my life—the turbulent peak experiences that threatened my very existence—which became my bridges from toughness to tenderness. Often our crises and tragedies are our most vital learning experiences in terms of personal growth. The Chinese character for the words "crisis" and "opportunity" is the same. Opportunities are disguised in most of our tragedies. Lost in pain, we fail to see them there.

These tragedies and peak experiences often enrich every life—every life not too numb to be void of all feeling. I'm speaking of crises such as the death of loved ones, rejection by others whom one values, failure and success in important endeavors, divorce, the pain and joys of love relationships and friendships, and the growth process afterwards which can enable one to do more than understand these events—to grow with them, to own them and the emotions which accompany them all.

Siddhartha, in the great book of that title by Hermann Hesse, found that it was impossible for him to help his son—as it is for us to help our friends, lovers, children, and students— to avoid the same mistakes he made in his life and that we all make in our lives.

It is only through struggling with the pain of our own crises, tragedies, sins, depressions, and problems that our greatness as human beings will be realized. Our crises are the anvils on which our growth is forged. And beneath the veneer of our tough shells lies the mother lode of the essence of us—our feelings and emotions, our tenderness.

It is very difficult to teach the value of crisis in a theoretical sense. It must be discovered. My crises overturned my entire overachiever world.

I first discovered the depth of the tenderness in me in 1969 during a crisis. I had just separated from my first wife after ten years of marriage, and I was on a lake in New Hampshire where I had spent all my childhood summers. The impact of the loss I was experiencing hit me full force. Usually when facing an emotional crisis, I had learned that I could outrun or outwit it by achieving something important, thus causing people to make a fuss over me.

On this occasion the emotional impact overcame me and I was immersed in my own anguish and loneliness. For the first time in my life I cried profusely. Beneath my protective shell I discovered part of the essence of myself—a creativity I had never suspected was there. I wrote a book and some poems, and I painted. Most importantly, I discovered a tender little boy part of me which had grown up at age five—a tenderness which I had never felt. I found to my surprise that, not only did my friends appreciate and love this tender little boy part of me better than the "perfect Hal" who always had it under control, but more importantly I myself loved this tender part. It was real, believable.

This was the beginning of a kind of "men's liberation" for me—a freeing from the macho toughness that I had thought was my strength, and an admission of the tenderness that I had thought to be my weakness, when it was really a strength.

Toughness Is Not Strength

The fact is, toughness is *not* strength. Toughness is a kind of brittleness. It is hard—until it meets a stronger force and has to yield. Then it crumbles, because it cannot yield, since people who think of themselves as "tough" also think of yielding as a sign of weakness. Thus, like the muscle-bound bodybuilder, such a person is locked inside a position of self-definition which does not serve *him*. He serves *it*. He is not "tough" at all. In fact, he is a slave to his own mind and to its idea of what strength is.

What is strength, then? My friend Gabriel Heilig offers this definition:

Strength is an impersonal quality. It is like a current, like water or electricity. It is always flowing. Whether it flows through *us* really depends on whether we are willing to surrender to it and become the vehicle for its flow. If we are willing to surrender, then we appear to be strong—and in fact we are strong, strong with the strength of Life that is always seeking to express itself in whatever form.

In trees, that strength takes the form of sturdy branches, deep roots, and many leaves. In a relationship, it may take the form of a powerful blending that allows the individuals involved to experience what strength feels like when it is *added* to strength.

Good friendships are like that, which is why they are so irreplaceable. Yet, whatever form strength may take, it always seems to have this same elusive and fascinating quality: it moves through us, and in a way it actually takes us over and *becomes* us, to the degree we can surrender to it. At the heart of being strong there is the paradox that the more we give up to this force the more of it we can express and experience in our own lives. But we can never own it, or make it "mine"—any more than we can steal it from anyone else. It belongs to no one, like the wind. And like the wind, it blows where it will. The way to catch it and to use it is to spread your sails for it to fill, not to puff out your chest as though it ever was yours.

I like this definition. It links strength to the entire life process, and locates it within that process. It captures the sense of grandeur and immensity that true strength always conveys to us, whether it is in the strong line of a piece of sculpture or in the sweep of an athlete's movement. Both artists and athletes admit without any shame that at their moments of greatest achievement it feels as if it is not they who are "doing" it. Some force seems to take them over and do it *through* them.

They often report that they actually feel like witnesses, observing this happening through them. By their practice and training, of course, they enable it to happen through them, but the important and really interesting thing is that these talented men and women actually report the distinct sensation that this strength or creative energy is literally moving *through* them, using their abilities as vehicles, much as electric current will use the guiding form of an insulated wire. Without the wire the electricity would exist, but we would not experience it or be able to use it. In the same way, we would never think to say that the wire "owned" the current, or that the wire itself was strong. What we would say and do say is that the wire is "high tension" —able to hold a high charge of this current.

I think this applies to people also. People who are strong are not necessarily the toughest, the biggest, or the loudest. Nor are they necessarily the ones who appear to be the most fearsome. Strength does not live on the outside of life. It lives within, and it moves from within. All good boxers know that the most effective punches are not the long, looping, obvious kayo punches that look so good in the movies. These punches look good, but they rarely land, because by the time they reach an opponent he has also seen them, and has ducked them easily. All they do is waste energy. The really effective punches are those which are swift, hard, and which travel the shortest distance. The opponent often does not see them coming, but he feels them when they land.

Films of Muhammad Ali fighting George Foreman prove this point. Before their fight, many sportswriters and other supposed experts were shaking their heads and wondering how Ali would ever stand up to Foreman's awesome firepower.

Ali didn't stand *up* to it. He stood inside its range as Foreman's punches whistled by like runaway locomotives outside the bedroom of a child under his blankets. Safe behind his guard along the ropes, Ali could easily see Foreman's slow, ponderous swings coming, and he had the time he needed to lean out of their way or step inside them. Ali's punches, on the other hand, were short, accurate, stinging—and they landed. They mystified Foreman, and then they mesmerized him. And finally, as we know, they toppled him, just as the short chopping swings of an axe will fell a huge oak.

Foreman may have been physically more powerful, yet it was Ali who was more supple and more flexible, and thus better able to allow the strength inside him to be expressed. His complete mastery over Foreman speaks for itself. As boxing experts now agree, Ali's victory was one of the most perfect exhibitions of boxing genius ever seen. Muhammad Ali won over George Foreman *not* because he was more powerful, for he was not. Ali won because he was more able to *use* his strength properly, to keep it inside him until the right moment and *then* let it out —not in wild bullying swings, but in fully conscious and guided tattoos, much like a riveter who picks his spots and then drills them. Thus, Ali made himself into a "high tension" instrument, able to contain his strength when it needed to be kept inside, and able also to release it fully and cleanly when the moment for that came.

His victory was not merely a triumph of muscles; it was a triumph of mind and of understanding. The margin of victory stemmed from the difference of understanding by each fighter about how to use his strength. It is an excellent example of what happens when a truly "tough" person confronts someone who "knows his own strength," as the old saying truly speaks of it.

In 1969, several years before Frederick Perls, who is noted for his work in Gestalt therapy, died, I met him at Esalen Institute. The brief exchange involved an introduction during which Perls and I shook hands, with me giving my habitual firm "military" handshake. Fritz Perls winced and withdrew his hand immediately, shouting, "Not so hard!" Somewhat shocked, I replied defensively, "Well, a good firm handshake, you know, is—" "Is a sign of weakness," interrupted Perls. "It's a cover-up for lack of warmth and sensitivity, which can be expressed in a gentle handclasp," which he proceeded to share with me in a most moving way. In the enlightening days that followed for me at Esalen, I was to learn a great deal more about my cover-ups, masks, and macho-ness, and my mistaken beliefs that toughness was strength.

So, toughness is not strength. Rather, toughness is a put-on quality, something that is added to what is already there in us, just as in the example of the person who feels he has to "build" his body.

Construction workers, athletes, and farmers all have strong bodies, but their bodies are grown naturally through the work they do. And their bodies are not "tough"—that is, hard—just for the sake of being hard. They become suited precisely to their lives. They appear to be in balance.

And, as we have seen, strength is an inner quality, a resource that most of us can find by going within ourselves and contacting those deeper sources of energy which swirl around human life like winds about the earth. Those winds do not belong to us, yet they do not mind if we spread our sails to let them carry us on toward our destinations. And there are few experiences more thrilling in life than to feel those healthy gusts blow across one's face, or through one's heart, and to know that one is being guided toward the goal that is completely right. Nature's strength is our strength, if we are willing to surrender our phony poses and let it enter us, and by living in us bring us that much nearer to its source.

No, toughness is not strength. It is weakness. And no, tenderness is not weakness. It is the door to greater strength. And the handle to the door lies within ourselves.

3 The Machismo Olympics

The other side of the trap of believing that toughness is strength is the assumption that anything *but* toughness *must* be a sign of weakness. This is not true, yet so many men—and a growing number of women—are afraid to display their "softer" emotions that it often *appears* to be true, and toughness comes to be equated with strength. However, toughness is *not* strength, as we have seen. It is brittleness.

From the time they begin to read, children in our society are bombarded with feedback about the appropriate behavior for them to exhibit as males or females. Feminist groups deserve applause from all of us for exposing the sexism in primary readers, TV programs, and textbooks. It is not at all uncommon for fathers unwittingly to drop the "man of the house" burden on their sons; that was my cross to bear.

And once high school age is reached, the athletic program, in spite of the many benefits it brings, seems to force the notion on the young male that he must become even tougher, that all males must be chauvinistic, that being a jock excludes being tender.

Hypermasculinity

Coaches, camp counselors, teachers, parents, our children—all of us are overly worried about sex-role behavior. There's this great fear that we might look or act as though we are homosexual, so we must all exaggerate our behavior as "men" so as to avoid that look. The fact is that this great polarization of homosexual and heterosexual roles is nonsense. No one is 100 percent heterosexual *or* homosexual, masculine *or* feminine. We are all human mixtures of the two, somewhere along a continuum which has pure femininity at one rare end and pure masculinity at the other (with almost no individuals at either pole).

According to Dr. Sandra Bem, a Stanford University psychologist, both hypermasculine men and hyperfeminine women usually think poorly of themselves—and they tend to score lower on IQ tests as well. Dr. Bem classified 1500 students by their stated preferences among a list of sixty traits, some very "masculine" (ambitiousness, assertiveness, self-reliance) and some most often thought of as "feminine" (being gentle, affectionate, and understanding).

One-third of the list was composed of qualities generally thought of as "neutral" (being friendly, likable, truthful). What Dr. Bem found was that the students who scored at the stereotyped extremes of both "masculinity" and "femininity" also scored far lower in self-assurance, higher in anxiety and neurotic conflict, and lower on IQ tests for spatial ability and creativity.*

Commenting on her findings, Dr. Bem speculated that her

*Sandra Bem, "The Measurement of Psychological Androgyny," *Journal of Consulting and Clinical Psychology* 42 (1974): 155–62; Bem, "Sex Role Adaptability: One Consequence of Psychological Androgyny," *Journal of Personality and Social Psychology* 31 (1975): 634–43.

results might indicate something about the rigid behavior patterns that people who identify themselves as only "masculine" or only "feminine" get locked and finally frozen into.

That we may exhibit traits of tenderness has no bearing on whether or not we are more homosexual than heterosexual (though many people who have been conditioned by sex-role stereotypes would have us think so). Accordingly, males are encouraged to put on a tough-guy mask to announce to all that we are definitely not "gay," but "straight." The more worried a young man may be about this supposed either-or dichotomy of homo- or heterosexuality or femininity, the more apt he is to overadvertise his maleness through macho behavior.

If men would liberate themselves from the great fear of homosexuality which is put upon them by our society, they could relax and be the *persons* they really are, persons who have both masculine and feminine qualities in their psychological makeup.

Those men who make the loudest demonstration of their maleness are usually very frightened human beings underneath, afraid of the tender or feminine feelings they possess. We men need a male liberation movement to help us free ourselves from the great pressures to be chauvinistic. Those pressures really hurt.

A strong man, "centered" enough to gain most of his approval from within rather than from external sources, can become comfortable enough with himself to have the courage to explore his own feelings about his masculinity/femininity. He can then accept these feelings as part of his total makeup and can determine where they fit in his life, rather than defending himself against these feelings by denial or by the schizoid behavior of splitting himself into two separate, numbly "behaving" personalities.

I had these anti-homosexual macho attitudes conditioned

into me to such a degree that I denied the tenderness in myself. This happens to many males. As I grew freer through some of my crises, I had several experiences which enabled me to explore and experiment about the masculine and feminine aspects of myself, and accordingly to accept the tender aspects in me as being wholesome and good. I was able to conclude comfortably that, though I was certain, after satisfying my curiosity, that I was predominantly a heterosexual male, I had some tender parts of me (usually inappropriately associated with homosexuality) which both my friends and I could value and enjoy. All of us need to be encouraged to have such freedom to experiment with and explore the most important subject in our universe—ourselves.

It is true that a century and more ago on the wild frontiers of America most men had to prove their virility continually in order to survive in their battle against nature, the Indians, and hostile gunmen.

The physical strength or toughness of the man in drawing and using his gun (his penis?) carried over to his relationships with the "weaker sex," whom he also had to conquer. In contrast to the brawling men, their women were dependent, weak, sweet smelling, and lace bedecked. (Or were they?) Now, over a century later, we are beginning to set aside the need to conquer our physical frontiers and are beginning to explore new emotional and spiritual frontiers—inner frontiers which cannot be assaulted in a head-on attack, but which may be more important to our lives as we evolve.

Machismo and Mortality

It seems so hard for men in our society to hug one another —to hug their fathers, brothers, or friends—and "hard" is an apt word for it, the way we stiffen up to avoid the warmth of body contact. This is also true of many women. The more I feel liberated as a human being, the more I also enjoy the experience of hugging some of my male friends with whom I feel close. However, there are few who are liberated enough to allow themselves and me this closeness without the stiff, armored back-slapping chest clash that so often suffices for a male hug. Males shake hands the same way. Some males are so out of touch that it is painful rather than pleasurable to shake hands with them, as they maul your hand in a viselike grip.

Strength, as we have seen, is a flowing energy, a flow which can be guided and directed consciously into particular areas or activities. Thus, a man with brute strength, like George Foreman, will be whipped by a man like Muhammad Ali, who can control and guide his strength. The man who will not relax, who will not let go of his tense pose as a tough hombre (a pose which takes a lot of energy to maintain), soon will become exhausted. His nerves will snap. He will develop ulcers and high blood pressure. When you think about it, it is no great wonder that the death rate among American business executives in the forty-to-fifty-five age bracket is growing so rapidly. By 1980, for every 650 men alive over the age of sixty-five, there will be 1000 women! American men feel they *must* keep up a constant show of readiness, a highly monitored display of stereotyped masculinity. Such a pose is all the harder to maintain, for not only must these men appear to be tough and hard-nosed, but they must also mask their macho attitudes beneath a veneer of studied politeness and proper protocols. They must be both savage and sophisticated, or they will soon be replaced by other men who can play the role better . . . for a few years, until *their* nerves collapse, and they too are replaced by younger men, who will burn themselves out in turn.

It is not a pretty picture. Beneath its surface comforts of fancy desks and fat expense accounts, American business is a

raw and battering jungle. Success in such a world is not characterized by strength but by power.

The recent successful publication of Michael Korda's *Power,*
which is a guide to success in the executive scramble, under-
lines the ever-present nature of threat in this world in which
the trappings of one's office can become symbols of intimida-
tion. For the executive who has "made it," no less than for the
junior scrambler on his way up, masculinity is generally not
something to hold inside oneself; it is something one must constantly display in outward shows of toughness. Men who are
promoted on the basis of such external equations of maleness
with toughness will go on to duplicate this pattern when they
select their replacements. In this way the bias toward a rigid
hierarchy of macho behavior will be institutionalized within a
large corporation, and the tone of its entire atmosphere will be
set.

The fears of a few men will spread to infect an entire office,
and move outward from there, until everyone in the company
is communicating the same meaningless macho noises, and the
tension builds, and the executives keep dying younger every
year.

The Price of Winning the Macho Olympics

The syndrome I am describing is not imaginary. It is all too
real, for all too many men. And few of the men afflicted by it
know how to stop reflecting it in their own behavior. So, afraid
to be judged "weak" by their superiors, they succumb and
submit to the unwritten law that all men must be tough all the
time.

This conspiracy of masculine imagery has now spread even
beyond the male jungle, politely referred to as "the business
world." Now women are clamoring—loudly and toughly—for

their entry into this grotesque carnival. They want equal rights in the corporate wars also. And to prove their worth, they are rapidly becoming as vicious and as brittle as many of their male counterparts. Indeed, many men find women to be even tougher than men as opponents. It is as if, sensing what they must do in order to succeed in a world dominated by the phony imagery of a one-sided masculinity, women have learned to mimic the external behaviors and cut-throat attitudes of this shadow game. It is hard to describe the strange power such women can possess; like the Hindu goddess Kali, they are both creators of life and its destroyers.

Some women are now reflecting the stereotyped aspects of male imagery in their own behavior. By doing this, they are holding the mirror up to men, to show us what we have looked like to them for so many years. It is not a very comforting glimpse. The lesson is there for any who care to read it: A world in which only "hard" feelings and behaviors are considered legitimate soon will annihilate itself. It is like a self-destruct machine. Such a pattern requires that more and more energy be poured into it. Yet what happens to that energy once it enters the system? It is not conserved, not kept inside, but is burned up quickly—partly through the constant display of toughness that is considered "strength," and partly through the high degree of nervous tension that is required to keep putting out so much toughness.

It is no wonder that business executives often eat and drink diets overloaded with meat and highly concentrated forms of protein and numbing alcohol, and that their whole beings are pervaded by this drive to be more and more concentrated, more and more tough, and more and more like machines—and less and less like the fluid and light-filled beings we really are.

The trap of toughness is all-consuming. The more energy is poured into this pose, the more energy is required to maintain it. Toughness rarely wins. It is always tense with the fear of losing.

Even in its moments of success toughness is steeling itself for the next battle. There is no end to it. The only end is death, a death that is usually harsh and sudden—not a bending, but a breaking. The brittle form no longer can hold the energy that is being poured through it, and it snaps. The heart bursts, the blood vessels break, the mind itself short-circuits.

The highest rates of suicide in the United States are for divorced businessmen around fifty years old, men who see themselves being hemmed in by younger male competitors, and who have left behind whatever security their families had provided. You can see them at business conventions, drinking with their "buddies," trying to look "tough," and hoping that some woman will make them forget, at least for a night, just how terribly vulnerable they are. Then, like Willy Loman in *Death of a Salesman,* it is back on the corporate bicycle, pedaling faster and faster to go nowhere at all.

What is missing in all of this is any sign of joy or contentment. In the Machismo Olympics no one is allowed to stop playing. "Men" never quit. Every macho knows that. Men whose ideal is to be "tough" cannot allow themselves to remain content for very long. For to be content would mean to give up the game, and for a macho the game is more important than anything else. A macho does not run the game of life—he is run by it.

In the Machismo Olympics no one is allowed to cop out. Every man must keep playing until he drops. And when he does drop, he is carried off the field by his children, who have been watching in horror, afraid to say a word for fear of being called sissy themselves.

There are no gold medals in the Machismo Olympics, but there are some trophies: promotions for some men (and heart attacks for others), a few affairs, a divorce or three, and along the way several children who cannot understand these men with whom they cannot communicate. These men are driven. For all their fantasies of power and control, they have none over themselves.

Their need for power is a reflection of the void they feel in their own lives. Their quest is empty, and it empties them. They have mortgaged their lives and their families' lives in order to worship at the altar of an image: tough, cool, and hard as Clint Eastwood when he pulls the trigger and his killer's grin curls silently as smoke around his cheroot.

The macho image is just that—an image. It is an idol, cold and empty. There is no aliveness in it. Quite the contrary, it devours the aliveness of any man (or any woman) who bows down to it, as many of us have learned. In the Machismo Olympics, there are no winners. There are only losers pretending they have won, and wondering why being tough hasn't been enough.

4 Tenderness: The Key to Strength

As we have seen, toughness is a compensation for a lack which is feared to exist. The man who is afraid that others may think he is not strong will come on tough; that way he hopes no one will question his act, and he will be accepted as a "real man." The man who is afraid to be intimate with women will come on like Superfly. He will score with many women but will allow no one to get close to him. His investment is in his image, while his real self goes unnourished, lonely between the blondes on either side. He is literally trapped in his own success, and for the sake of his public image as a playboy he will not give it up. He will not abandon his act.

This seeming inability to acknowledge one's act and to give it up means that more and more of a person's energy will go into keeping the pretense up and into adjusting the images he has created for the world's approval. But we are not these images. Images are static. People are fluid. Yet, so many of us have trouble giving up our precious self-*images* and accepting our *selves*.

How can we get from image to self? How can we stop being *stuck* and start being *source?* These are some of the questions this book seeks to explore.

We have seen that true strength is not a commodity that can be owned the way one owns a pair of shoes. Strength is a quality, an active force in the world. *It is in the world already.* We do not have to create it.

What we have to do is to get in touch with it. We do not have to *own* the strength we want to use. We have to *connect* with it. And in order to do that, we have to be open to it. A wise teacher has said, "If you go to the ocean with a thimble, you will come away with a little water. If you go with a bucket, you will come away with more." What we get depends on how open we are. The more open we are, the more we can accept. The more rigid and closed off we are, the less can enter us. As Norman Mailer has put it, the law of life is simple: "Either we grow or we pay more for staying the same."

Whether we grow or whether we get stuck depends on our openness. Strength means nothing unless we also have a way to release and to use it.

In order to win the Kentucky Derby, more than a fast horse is needed. A good jockey is also needed. The jockey is far smaller than the horse he rides, yet without him the horse's speed and strength will be wasted.

In the same way, all of us need something more than mere strength in order to be successful in our lives. We need a way to tap our strength. Otherwise it will remain a hidden treasure buried within us, while our dreams and daydreams taunt us with thoughts of "what we could have been if only . . ." If only we had known how to *get at* it.

How *do* we get at our strengths?

Don't Push the River

There is a useful story which helps to reveal the answer. Not long ago a track coach told his sprinters to run their practice heats flat out, so that he could time them at what they felt was their absolute top speed. The runners ran their heats, and the coach recorded their times. Then he told them to run another heat, this time putting out only 80 percent of their energy. The runners ran again. The results were astounding: In every case each runner had actually improved on what he felt was his best effort! They all ran faster when they tried less hard.

What this true story tells us is that we do have to surrender into our strength for it to flow through us. It *is* there, already, inside us. Forcing it only pushes it further away. Someone who forces life also is going to be frustrated by life.

Someone who can relax and let life move through him will be sustained and rewarded by it. He will not have to worry about forcing life to give him what he needs; it will just come. As the great Chinese sages taught, "Sitting quietly, doing nothing, everything is achieved." And the Zen saying aptly warns, "Don't push the river."

Looking at things this way, we can see that perhaps we do not have to hammer life (or ourselves) over the head in order to get what we need or want. Perhaps we can flow with the river of life instead of swimming against the current, and trust that what we need will come to us. This is a risky-sounding piece of advice to most Americans. We are not taught to trust this way. We are taught instead to "try our best" and "never quit." Yet perhaps trying hard is not the whole answer. To use the illustration of the sprinters, they were trying when they ran both heats; but in the first heat they were trying 100 percent, and in the second heat they only tried 80 percent. They didn't give up altogether, or wait for a gust of wind to carry them down the track. They ran, they put out effort, but they let the running carry them, so to speak; they didn't exert force against their muscles while they were doing it. As a result they ran faster.

In the same way, we can see that strength needs to be unlocked in order to be fully effective. There is a difference between controlling our strength and guiding it.

An irrigation ditch doesn't control the flow of water into a cotton field; it can't tell the rain when to fall or not to fall. Likewise, many artists and creative geniuses in all fields, including the sciences, report that at the moment of their greatest achievements they felt as though they had been filled by an immense creative force. They could not control this force, but through their skill and insight they were able to guide and to express it.

I'm not willing to accept that science and technology should seek dominance over nature and control over nature's laws. One can't be superior to nature. The way to work with natural (or supernatural) phenomena is not to stand apart from them and try to penetrate their secrets through violence, but rather to be a part of nature and be reverently devoted to her.

I love nature (part of what I feel to be my Indian heritage), and when I am in the woods, I find that if I try *hard* to catch a deer it will not come to me. If, however, I meditate on being at one with the deer, seeing the deer with "soft eyes," the deer comes to me as I become one with the deer. It has become a mystical and ceremonial experience for me. One might ask how such hunting can be tender. Some of you will know the answer. For others I can only assure you that there is a dramatic difference between this kind of hunting and the more macho variety. I have done both.

Several years after I began this blending way of being with

wild animals, I found that my Tlingit Indian brethren also have practiced it for years. I have been told that I am a Tlingit Indian by reincarnation. This is quite different from being an honorary Indian, which is an honor that occasionally an Indian tribe will bestow upon someone who has made a special contribution. The Tlingits have told me that I *was* a Tlingit Indian named Doox in a former life, and now that this has been recognized and identified by a great chief of the Tlingit tribe, David Abraham (who died at the age of 103), I have burial and fishing rights on a river in Yakutat, Alaska.

The belief is that either the spirit of a deceased Tlingit will enter the body of a chosen person, thus bringing about the reincarnation of the Indian spirit, or the Indian's spirit will be reborn in the chosen person. The Tlingit chief who identified me had several clues as to my identity, one of which was my prowess as a fisherman and hunter and my unrestrained enthusiasm, mixed with tenderness, toward nature—traits shared by Doox, who, he said, I had been in a past life. As soon as the word spread among my Tlingit people, the usual hostility toward the white man vanished and I was embraced as a brother.

Accepting and flowing with this spiritual phenomenon, after having for so much of *this* life been closed to the possibility of such a spiritual reality, has been a vitally important experience for me. To be open to the possibility that I have been and am a Tlingit Indian and that I possess strengths that some other white men do not is a transforming and beautiful experience for me. It is a part of my life now to become part of nature rather than to understand or control her.

The Opening and the Barring of the Door

The *Wen Fu,* an ancient Chinese prose-poem on the art of letters, acknowledges the mystery of this flow:

> This thing which is in me but which
> no efforts of mine can slay!
> Wherefore time and again I stroke
> my empty bosom in pity for myself:
> so ignorant am I of what causes the
> opening and the barring of the door.

Lu Chi, the author of the *Wen Fu,* was ignorant, over 1700 years ago, and we are ignorant today. We have traveled to the moon and to Mars, yet we have not penetrated very far inside the human heart. It is our own inner space that is the next and the most challenging frontier for the adventurous among us.

The author of the *Wen Fu* admits that he is ignorant of what causes "the opening and the barring of the door." Yet such admissions are the beginning of wisdom. To know that we do not know is to know a great deal. To realize that "the opening and the barring of the door" of inspiration is a mystery and not a mechanical procedure gives us an important clue in our search for the key that *will* allow us to connect with our true inner strengths.

My not knowing that I was a Tlingit Indian, and yet becoming open enough to flow with that possibility, opened the door rather than barred it to this "new reality" for me.

When we are dealing with a mechanical process, there is little choice but to become mechanical ourselves. That is the most appropriate and useful response. But when we are dealing with a process which remains even today a mystery, then we must adopt a different attitude. Neither how-to books nor rote behavior will do. Some measure of respect, and even of spiritual reverence, is required. There must be complete attention as the door slowly opens. We cannot yank on the handle and pull it open. If we do, the inspiration or the strength we seek will only disappear back into the darkness. We must treat these forces lovingly, and with a certain tenderness, or they will be lost to us.

It may seem strange to speak of tenderness as the key to releasing one's inner strengths, yet I feel that this is in fact how we *do* release these subtle inner forces. Even a weight lifter, to take an obvious example of strength, must treat his body tenderly, or he will make little progress in his sport. He cannot punish his body by forcing it to lift heavy weights all at once. Body strength is the result of cumulative exercise, not one or two exhausting sessions in the gym. Such sessions are only that —exhausting. Exhausting the body is not strengthening it. Successful athletes achieve success through patient work, slowly building the tolerance of the entire body, so that a maximum result is achieved with minimum strain. Strain is not strength. It is punishment against the self, and it reduces the body's ability to release its own strength.

Even in the actual weight-lifting competition, any good weight lifter knows that there is far more to his sport than brute strength alone. To be successful, one must have more than big muscles. Split-second coordination and an intimate knowledge of the body's limits and tolerances are also required. The body can be stretched and strained, but if it is overstrained it will react; muscles will pull, or even tear, and years of training will be rendered useless in an instant. As he is lifting, the weight lifter must be able to stay in tune with the feedback his body is giving him, so that he knows when to make his move, when to kick his legs out to brace himself for the final push upward. Even as he is testing his body, he must be gentle with it—not touchy, but gentle: tender. He must respect its limits as well as its strength. If he does not, he will do what so many careless athletes have done; he will burn it out.

This example of the weight lifter is an extreme one, yet even here we can see how absolutely necessary it is to be in touch with and tender toward our sources of strength. For the weight lifter, that source is located in his muscles. For the photographer, in his sense of vision, space, and color. For the race driver, in his depth perception and reflexes. For the mountaineer, in his balance, stamina, and timing. In every activity where strength is required, sensitivity also is required. Without it the strength will remain in its raw state as brute force.

It will not be refined for use by the conscious intelligence.

What refines our strength is its complement tenderness. Strength and tenderness both must be present if we are to make full use of our potentials. We must be strong if we are to explore the full range of our capabilities, and we also must be tender if we are to give them full expression.

But what *is* tenderness?

I believe that tenderness is more than speaking softly or being pliant. That is the stereotyped view of tenderness, and like many stereotypes it contains an essential element of truth. Yet I think that tenderness is a much more subtle quality, one to which men in particular have paid far too little attention over the years, in the false assumption that strength and toughness were all they needed. Now we are beginning to see that strength and toughness by themselves do not accomplish very much. Even a moon rocket goes nowhere without its internal monitoring and guidance systems. The engines of these rockets possess an incredible capacity to release power; yet, for this very reason, they require the closest attention and the most delicate fine tuning. A slight error can result in an enormous catastrophe. Human beings (would you believe) are more powerful than moon rockets.

The human organism can receive, transmit, and transform an incredible amount of raw force. We do it all the time. We take in sunlight, water, food, sense impressions, informal and emotional communications from other people—and we transform these inputs into work, creative ideas, art, families, and the whole fabric of human society. It is a miracle, yet most of us never stop to acknowledge this for what it really is. To many of us, perhaps, it all seems very humdrum and even very boring. We look for something "exciting" in our lives. If we only could experience the magic we perform every day, we might begin to realize that something truly extraordinary is at work in our lives. For what we do is to take the elements that are present around us in our environment, and transform these into entirely new structures: cars, houses, libraries and the books in them, even moon rockets. All are the creations of human beings. Without the ability of the human intelligence to transform its environment, it would hardly change except for seasonal alterations and natural catastrophes. What is more, human beings have the capacity to be aware of their own abilities and conscious processes—and to transform these—while they are occurring. This ability is more than survival oriented. It is evolutionary.

Being tender is one key to this power-of-transformation by which the self reaches its own source and taps this immensely creative strength that is alive within it. It is a strength which is abundant in men as well as women. By liberating the woman in every man, and the man in every woman, we will all take one giant step toward realizing our own vast human potential.

Natural Male Aggressiveness

In speaking of the importance of men reclaiming their tenderness, I want to be careful not to create the impression that I am suggesting that men become passive or give up what I would call a natural male aggressiveness. This is a difficult and delicate distinction to make. On the surface, a man who exhibits natural male aggressiveness in his relationships with women may not appear tender. Yet this is not necessarily the case. Nor am I making a case for sexless relations between men and women. It is the natural yin and yang differences between the sexes that are one source of the mutual pleasure between men and women—sexual and otherwise. It would be a mistake to attempt to erase the fact that men are usually heavier, stronger, and built more solidly than women—or to pretend that women are not generally softer, curvier, and softer-voiced than men.

Perhaps an example which presents itself to me while I am in the woods can help me explain this more adequately. During the mating, or "rut," season the male deer becomes more aggressive instinctively as he prepares to mate and propagate the species. Now, the doe also wants to mate and propagate the species with as strong an instinct and desire as the buck.

But why, then, does she run from him, leading him on a chase through the woods? Why, since they both have this desire, do they play "the game" of the male aggressively pursuing the female?

I don't know the answer to this question. It's one of nature's mysteries, but I do know that it is the natural way for them. When the buck catches the doe, then the mating has an incredible (yet still aggressive) tenderness to it somehow. The doe stops evading. It is part of a drama—a game played out. You never, *never* see a doe chasing a buck during the rut. Nor do you see them mate without the little chasing game of buck after doe.

When I was in my college years, we males pursued and "chased" our girl friends in this same courting game that the deer play so naturally. Some of it was so much macho bunk, a game played to impress our friends that we were strong and virile. Those who made the biggest display of the game were usually those who had the biggest personal doubts about their own sexual powers or virility. On the other hand, there is something natural about the human male aggressive sexual role, as there is with the bucks and does, something that I do not want to pretend isn't naturally there. Somehow, the *naturalness* in the male aggressiveness preserves the delicate tenderness in it.

It is the unnatural or *exaggerated* aspects of aggressiveness in some males which causes the unfortunate shift from tenderness to toughness.

The buck never does harm to the doe in his sexual aggressiveness. For example, he never mates when she is not ready—in heat. He is very tender in this regard, and men can learn from this. The buck is aggressive when the doe is ready for him to be, and somehow he knows when she is ready—in spite of her fleeing from him. The same can be true for aware and tender men and women. The doe is not fleeing in fear or terror but as a part of her desire, her part of the natural game.

Women who have assumed the *male* aggressive role sexually are not feminine, tender, or attractive to me. Some women may react negatively to this statement. I do not mean that I do not enjoy a woman taking the initiative in sexual play or activity. I find that, at times, such female initiative is not only very natural but refreshing. In fact, it is at times *unnatural* for the woman to *not* take the initiative.

The doe actually takes the initiative in the sexual process with the buck, in that it is *her* coming into heat that triggers the entire rutting or mating process, rather than *his* desire. She also takes some added initiative by periodically visiting and hanging out at his "scrapes." (The buck scrapes several places free of leaves on the ground, urinates on them, and leaves one hoofprint in the middle of each as his mark or calling card. These scrapes delineate the boundaries of his territory to mark his turf both for the does to visit and as a stay-away warning for other bucks.) The doe visits these scrapes when *she* is ready, yet *she* still leads the buck on the chase. And her running is no phony ploy. He really must run to catch her. He indicates to her through his ability to catch her that he is really interested, that he is a healthy and a worthy sire for her fawn. So much is communicated by this natural dance of male-female energies.

In *my* youth, many young women *knew* when they were attractive and when young men really wanted them by our willingness to pursue them aggressively in the courting game. Though we have gained some good things through our more liberated attitudes toward sex, particularly for women, we have in some ways thrown out the baby with the bath water. I do not want to contribute to a polarized notion that men must give up their natural sexual aggressiveness in order to be tender, and that women must take over the male aggressive role and give up their natural sexual tenderness or femininity. We males can still stake out our territory, leave our marks as territorial signals for women to heed and other men to be cautious about. We can still play nature's spontaneous courting game. There can still be a natural chase of sorts, and it can end, *if* it is *naturally* played, in a tender and beautiful union.

Changes in values and in the times have created widespread confusion among the several generations which now inhabit our planet. It is no wonder that we remain confused and bewildered about what our natural roles are—or were. So we attempt to play out roles in this great drama of life in the ways that we think we are *expected* to play them. The naturalness then disappears from the game. We are seeking approval from external sources rather than from within—environmental support rather than self-support. There is a vital need to "center ourselves" in these times of fast-changing values. We need to look within ourselves for our natural flow and inner rhythms which can help free us to be the uniquely beautiful male and female human beings we are. The process of therapeutic growth—our work on ourselves, our tender exploration into our inner frontiers—is one important way to regain our inner child's awareness of these basic rhythms. The game for us to play or flow through is the *natural* one.

The unnatural game that we play because we think we

should play it really is a trap. This is a game called "Let's Play a Game and Pretend We Are Not Pretending We Are Playing One." The sad thing is that we numb ourselves to a point where we forget we are pretending and then wonder why it's so unnatural and unfulfilling.

Tenderness is a natural flowing process for both men and women, and it doesn't mean that men cannot still be naturally aggressive.

Additionally, we men need to be careful that we do not play the unnatural game of pretending we are tender just to gain the approval of others. There is an ample reservoir of natural tenderness within all of us males. Tenderness is really naturalness. And our own personal journey toward our inner selves will reveal this to us.

5 Therapeutic Growth: Real-izing Our Potential

Most of us realize only 5 to 15 percent of our potential in our lifetimes—a tragic waste of ourselves. To the degree that we have a fixed approach, a rote set of responses to things, we limit ourselves to a small fraction of our potential. The macho man, playing his supermale role, is set in a fixed approach to life and to others. To the degree that we are spontaneous—here and now—reacting in the moment, we have much more of our potential available. This nourishes spontaneity rather than a rote "behavior."

The liberated male or female is one who can respond spontaneously without fear of censure or ridicule, since he or she is becoming free of the slavish need for the "shoulds" or approval of most others. Such liberated persons have far more of their potential available. Yet, most of our schools and academic institutions teach us to respond with a fixed behavior. The entire lecture mode of teaching, with students regurgitating back on exams exactly what the teacher has said and being rewarded with grades, is an all too common example of this external rather than internal approval.

The person who is in touch with his or her own spontaneity is free to be tender, feminine, or masculine in his or her responses, since he or she is not hung up on playing the appropriate role. Not trusting his own inner rhythms, but rather relying on external cues from others about what his responses should be—and getting cues that they should be clearly masculine, or tough, and thus not tender—the average male steels or tightens himself up as protection from others and from his own spontaneity. "Control yourself!" means stiffen yourself and, eventually, "Numb yourself" from any spontaneity. It is a heavy price to pay for "being a man."

The strongest males I know are also tender persons. One of the saddest experiences of my life was losing a best friend who was killed when he was relatively young. I took his two young pre-teen daughters for a walk around a lake to help console them for the loss of their father and to share with them how much I cared for him, too. I told them that I knew that I would cry at his funeral the next day and that many others would also and I hoped that they would feel free to cry. The twelve-year-old said, "Daddy wouldn't want me to cry." I told her that I knew he would, that the strongest men I knew cried on occasions and he was one of the strongest men I ever knew. I shared with them the fact that he and I had cried together several times. We all had tears of great grief those next few tragic days, and I know I emerged with more vitality for living as a result of fully experiencing the loss of my friend—a tender yet very strong man.

Chinks in Our Body Armor

Eventually the bodies of many of us undergo major changes, changes that are difficult to undo without a process of therapeutic growth. The growth process, which is not necessarily found in therapy, might involve a variety of peak experiences or psychotherapy. Often it involves direct body therapy. The immobilization of the body is the "body armor" that Wilhelm Reich and Alexander Lowen have spoken of, defenses that we build up to protect ourselves from others: from attack, from hostility, and, ultimately and most unfortunately, from our own feelings—feelings we so often mistrust and from which we alienate ourselves.

The chest of the macho male is tight. Its breathing is restricted and shallow, which is a natural numbing defense against painful feelings.

The shoulder muscles are tense and often hunched up; the buttocks are held in tightly—the expression "a tight-ass" is an accurate one! The leg muscles are tense, and the chest is puffed out to exaggerate a look of virility. This is the uptight posture which often becomes chronic in the average macho male. Feelings and emotions are restricted and held tightly within; very little, if any, tenderness is acceptable or physically possible in such a body.

This tightening of the body often has important corresponding psychological and attitudinal effects on the person. For example, what in my formal military world used to be praised as excellent military bearing I have since discovered to be a habitual and defensive immobilization of the body, and often the personality as well. A healthy, integrated individual is one who is both physically and emotionally capable of free flow, energy exchange, and movement. Without its corresponding physical freedom, emotional freedom is hardly possible. There are a variety of effective body therapies which can be integrated with the psychological work the individual needs to do. The work of Ida Rolf ("Rolfing"), Alexander Lowen, Wilhelm Reich, and Moshe Feldenkrais comes to mind immediately. Unfortunately, however, many of the disciples of these masters are better guides for the technical body work than they are for the more complex and essential psychological work.

When only the chronic body armor and defenses are corrected, the causes of them—the psychological wounds—are often left sticking out like sore thumbs.

Therapeutic Growth Toward Tenderness

When I speak of "therapeutic growth," I would like to make it clear that I do not mean only formal psychotherapy, though I would include that as one process under the larger umbrella. Therapeutic growth is any process leading toward realization of our greater human potential, be it through psychotherapy, crises, est, academic work, marriage, or other relationships which integrate physical, intellectual, emotional, and spiritual development.

Is therapeutic growth an essential path to tenderness for the hard-core macho male? I've been speaking of therapeutic growth as though I take it for granted that it is *the* way to grow from the numbness of toughness to the awareness of tenderness. I do consider that, in this world of great alienation from our bodies, feelings, and one another, some kind of personal growth work is vital if a person is to correct the havoc so often inflicted by a no doubt well-meaning society of parents, schools, and academic institutions. The popular book *I'm O.K., You're O.K.*, by Thomas A. Harris, M.D., illustrates clearly that even the best parents cannot bring up a child who will be free of the "I'm not O.K." attitude in which many of us spend so much time.

I often advise people to question entering into a long-term relationship with someone who has not undergone some significant therapeutic growth experiences. Perhaps the best twenty-first-century dowry that a young woman or man will bring to a marriage, if that institution as we know it today even survives the present century, will be several years of positive growth experiences.

Therapeutic growth is the freeing process of maturing, or growing from environmental to self-support. Freedom is a growing away from external approval of parents, teachers, bosses, therapists, and society to genuine internal approval from within ourselves. With this freedom comes the ability to be the naturally tender persons we all were as infants before we had to protect ourselves from hostile environments. Our growing can enable us to respond spontaneously and appropriately.

Life is too short and precious to spend it always numbly prepared for the barrage of hostile elements which will come at times, but which are often remote. And when they are remote, we could be savoring and sharing our tenderness with other special people if we would only drop our guards. Therapeutic growth enables us to respond appropriately, to have the strength of our potential and the strength of our tenderness available when appropriate.

The Neurotic Normal

Yet let me also make it clear that I am speaking principally of therapeutic growth for *normal* "neurotic" human beings, and that I feel that most of us fit this classification. In today's world, so many of us fear that our being "out of step" is an indication of our strangeness rather than the strangeness of society. The so-called neurotic person is the *natural* product of this society. It is not just our parents who are at fault. They, too, are helpless victims of our society.

I also am *not* suggesting that the goal of therapeutic growth is to make better-"adjusted" individuals who will "adapt" to society. We have a surplus of "well-rounded" people who "role" in whatever direction they are pushed. Perhaps we need more "square" people rather than rolling or "ruling" ones, who have the courage to stand fast or stand at all. The gifted individual who possesses exceptional stores of creativity and originality which demand expression is often blocked by lockstep institutions and a conformist society, and he is labeled "weird." This is the "neurotic normal" I speak of, whose tenderness hardens to a shell when repeatedly wounded.

The goal of the therapeutic growth I am speaking of is to free us to be spontaneous, creative, fulfilled individuals—to sever the bonds which enslave us to external approval, to the "shoulds" of those who are so quick to pretend to know what is best for us. In a sense I am advocating a revolution of the self—a revolution that does not espouse the tearing down of society and others through its toughness, but instead leads the way to the inherent strength in our own tenderness and the fostering of warmth in interpersonal relations which can grow through such "disarmament." If such a revolution does not take place soon, our society will be headed into an age of feelinglessness.

We have only our own potential to gain, that 85 percent of ourselves which so few of us ever venture into: new realities and possibilities which society may not know about and certainly won't appreciate as we become less predictable. So I am not saying that to rediscover our tenderness we must have formal therapy. Therapeutic growth is the process of growing, however it takes place. If you can afford a good therapist, formal therapy is one route. However, good therapists are so difficult to find that it takes some careful looking and some good luck. There is no correlation between academic background, accreditation, or licensing and effective therapists.

Psychiatrists—Overtrained and Underlived

Some people consider it safer to seek out psychiatrists, who are M.D.'s, rather than psychologists, who needn't be—and usually this *is* safer. It may be so safe, however, that after five years and tens of thousands of dollars, the individual will be forever "cured"—cured of rocking society's boat or making waves of any kind.

Being "cured" often is synonymous with being tamed. In the delightful book *The Little Prince,* by Antoine de Saint-Exupéry, the fox explained that if the little prince tamed him, he, the fox, would always need the little prince. It is no wonder many patients prefer their state of neurosis or psychosis to the drabness of "adjusted" normality.

Certainly there are good psychiatrists, as there are good psychologists. But being a psychiatrist does not insure that one has the traits vital to a good therapist. In fact, if the good psychiatrist still has these traits, it may well be in spite of his decade or more of traditional education and training. Psychiatrists strong enough to survive that grueling training and still trust their own inner rhythms and feelings will have had to unlearn much of the traditional theory they were taught, had to get out and just *experience* their lives. They must be human to be effective. They are not "therapy machines." Those don't work.

Psychiatrists have had to put so much time, energy, and money into their tedious preparation that they are often understandably eager to begin practice; and the tragedy is that this is usually before they have had the opportunity to gain real-life experience. So they often begin a financially successful practice, insulated all day long in the cocoonlike environment of the office, where there are few opportunities for them to take any of the real risks (except vicariously through their patients).

Thus, they remain isolated from the failures, crises, joys, and tragedies which are often the stimulus to personal growth.

I experienced several years of psychotherapy with such a psychiatrist, whom I liked as a human being, but whom I eventually left when I realized that *his* excitement in life really consisted of what he gained vicariously by living *my* adventures and those of his other patients from his plush office-apartment. I was paying him forty dollars an hour for this! Yet, in a way, it was a tribute to his skill and to my own progress that I eventually became strong enough to see this, and to leave him.

What really matters for you in a therapist, far more than degrees or licenses, is the depth of his or her experience and how he or she has grown through the challenges and crises of life. Has your therapist merely played around on the periphery of life, staying in the safety of the theoretical shadows, or has he or she lived boldly in the sunlight and darkness, expanding ego boundaries and consciousness? That is the really crucial question to consider in selecting a therapist.

Traits of the Effective Therapist

Carl Rogers has done some excellent research on what traits are present in the effective therapist. He and his associates have also found that these traits are present in the effective teacher or "learning facilitator," as he likes to call teachers. I'm convinced that these traits also contribute to effectiveness in most walks of life. I'd certainly value them in any mate or friend.

The first trait is *genuineness*, or the ability to be yourself, to be real, and not put on a mask and play the role of a therapist or wear an image of perfection. Genuineness is a human trait. Human beings are not perfect; that status is reserved for gods, and all one has to do is observe a handicapped child to realize that even God is far from perfect. There are no gurus, except the guru in oneself.

The second trait present in the effective therapist is *empathy*, the ability to put yourself in the other's shoes. A therapist who hasn't lived much of life and who hasn't experienced much therapeutic growth himself will have trouble putting himself into *your* crises and tragedies.

The third trait is a sense of *prizing* other human beings—caring about them, valuing them to the point of celebrating their uniqueness. Beware of the therapist who really doesn't seem to care about people. A healthy person or therapist takes care of himself—and is also willing to extend that care to others. Beware the therapist who seems bored by you and your struggle. He probably *is* bored. Him you don't want.

The fourth trait is a sense of *trust* which develops and grows between the therapist and patient. I find that this trait flows largely from the other three.

These are the four traits that Carl Rogers' research has shown to be present in the effective therapist.

As I've indicated, I would also want my therapist to have lived life deeply. I would want to know if his practice of therapy was an important and vital experience for him *and* for his patients. The best therapists I have experienced have exhibited these traits, and thus have helped me to acquire them also. Boredom breeds boredom. Aliveness breeds aliveness. It is *your* therapy. Choose for *your* self.

Follow No Master Too Far, Other Than the Master Within Yourself

The best therapists are not from one camp of therapy or another. They are themselves—unique, complex human beings. Their approaches are eclectic, drawn from the best of those other approaches which, when integrated with their own particular strengths, offer a unique stimulus to therapeutic growth for their clients. I feel the best therapists, and their patients, follow no master too far, other than the master within themselves. They use their own natural strengths and integrate these with the skills they have gained. I am most effective in helping others to grow when I am following my own rhythms most, using my own natural strengths rather than following a Fritz Perls, a Carl Rogers, or a Shelly Kopp.

Shelly Kopp, a therapist I respect immensely, never accepts a patient unless he feels the person will probably become important to *him* personally and give *him* something in return. I like Shelly's selfishness. Life is too short and too important to spend eight hours a day working with people from whom you get nothing but money. Money is not aliveness.

The traits of the effective therapist are not the kinds of skills that are usually found in classrooms or books. One must discover these traits in life. Fertile environments can be created in which we can begin to discover empathy, genuineness, prizing, and trust; but mainly we must *live* life, succeeding and failing at important endeavors and relationships, stumbling and then getting up again, loving and losing loves, to grow closer toward wisdom in our journeys through life.

The process of therapeutic growth offers many different paths, all leading toward the same awareness and its inherent tenderness toward ourselves and others. Psychotherapy is one of these paths, and there are many psychotherapeutic paths, but all of them are only as effective as you and your respective therapist want to make them. The menu of therapies offering you a path down the road of enlightenment today is enough to confuse people. If you wish to explore the path to your own liberation through therapy, shop around for a while. Talk to others you respect who have experienced several therapists and several types of therapy. Read some of the many books available. It's a consumer's market and you are the consumer.

Once you begin, however, recognize that you are beginning

a journey down "a path with heart," a path which involves risk. The more courage you have to take the risks of being adventurous, vulnerable, and tender, the greater your gains can be.

Because there are so many paths, many people today are trying them all, waiting for "it" to happen to them as soon as they stumble onto the best way. "It" doesn't happen to you. You grow gradually by putting your heart and soul and energy into the work. Just as the woman who isn't having orgasms sometimes flits from man to man, searching for a "better man" to give her an orgasm, when the key to her orgasm lies within herself, some people flit from therapist to therapist and from therapy to therapy searching for the right one to unlock their enlightenment, when that key is within themselves.

Taking responsibility for yourself is the cornerstone of *any* good therapy. *You* get the credit for all your gains in therapy, not the therapist. *You* also are responsible for all your problems. You own them, even if parents and nightmarish environments contributed to your having them. It is up to you and you alone to do something about yourself. Until you are ready to face taking responsibility for yourself and your growth, therapy will give you little. Do not enter formal therapy just because someone else or this book suggests it. Enter because *you* are ready to take responsibility for working toward your own therapeutic growth.

When you are ready to change, you will begin to take steps to change. It is senseless for parents or mates to try to force a son or daughter or a friend or mate to go to a therapist. Few good therapists would ever take such a patient. Discover your own need to grow. Make that decision yourself. It is a vitally important first step toward taking responsibility for your life.

Therapeutic growth, which is really growing through the process of life itself, offers paths to enlightenment and tenderness other than individual therapy or the accidental working-out of life's ups and downs. In some situations group therapy is more efficient, economical, and effective than individual therapy. At times a combination of individual therapy work on deeply personal childhood problems offers an excellent base for work in a group setting on interpersonal relations with other members. The group offers a powerful context difficult to achieve in an individual one-to-one setting. The infectious nature of one person's achieving a breakthrough in front of the others triggers reactions that might take months to achieve in individual therapy. Besides this, opening yourself and taking responsibility in the presence of others is more emotionally powerful, which tends to make such experiences and insights more indelible and long-lasting. In addition, occasional weekend encounter sessions or groups with effective leaders can provide the opportunity to explore a variety of different approaches, which together can have a cumulative releasing effect. When this work is followed up with ongoing therapeutic growth work, often it can be very useful.

Some see fit to seek enlightenment through therapeutic growth in yoga, meditation, est, martial arts, and the numerous other movements which have appeared upon the scene, many of which stem from ancient practices or religions which have revived in popularity in the past few decades. Others seek consciousness expansion through work with various gurus, diets, or drugs. It is not always the particular practice or technique that makes the real difference. More importantly, it is the individual's desire and commitment to work and the quality of his or her therapist or teacher.

Who Knows When Therapy Should End?

How long should therapy last? Until the patient is ready to end it. Only the patient will know when that time comes. When

formal therapy ends, the process of therapeutic growth continues. Enlightenment and tenderness do not occur overnight. It
takes time to undo the nightmares of childhood, the injustices
of school, and the depersonalization of society, and to soften the
callous shells of the macho male and the out-of-touch female so
they can trust others enough to be exposed and vulnerable. It
takes time to discover for yourself those freeing truths which
may be very apparent to the therapist or to others who relate
with you. It would be a big mistake for the therapist to try to
tell you these truths, robbing you of the discovery of them, clear
as they may be to him or her.

Often the truths are too elusive and simple for the patient
to hear or read about. They must be discovered through experience. Even understanding them is not enough.

Frequently the patient becomes confused and attempts to
program his or her way out of the confusion, which usually leads
to even more confusion. Confusion results when we are stuck
at an impasse between polarities—masculine/feminine, strong/
weak, good/bad, tender/tough. If we stay with our confusion,
answers will often emerge on their own. The fact is that we are
all of these things—good/bad, tender/tough, masculine/femi-
nine. And owning these polarities is part of the liberation we are
seeking—the liberation from always being good, or masculine,
or feminine, and feeling guilty when we do not live up to such
impossible expectations or "shoulds."

How long will our therapeutic growing process take? It's to
be hoped, all our lives, if we remain aware, alive human beings.
But when do we end the formal therapy with the therapist?
When the patient begins to be in touch with good things about
himself and about his therapist, he might think he would like
to continue forever. But eventually he discovers that the therapist is as human as he is, that the therapist has no answers that
he does not have within himself. As he becomes more "cen-

tered," he realizes that he is beginning to "see" answers for himself that the therapist does not see. He realizes that together he and the therapist have been growing and discovering and that they are on a journey together that could continue forever. The Leonard Cohen song makes the point well:

> "Have I carved enough, my Lord?"
> Child, you are a bone! . . .
> "Oh teachers are my lessons done?"
> Or must I learn another one?
> They laughed and laughed and said,
> "Are your lessons done? Are your
> lessons done?"

When we, "the patients," discover at last (and we'll need to keep rediscovering this over and over again because we will forget and regress again and again) that the therapist is not a master, that we must decide ourselves when we've "carved enough" and when our lessons are done, that there are no masters, that no one else has a secret charm to get us to the heart of this or any other matter, then where else do we have to look except within ourselves?

6 Tenderness Toward the Self

Learning to Say No

Each of us—particularly if we are a parent, a student, a busy executive, a teacher, or for that matter any kind of conscientious human being—is pulled in many directions by conflicting demands. It is virtually impossible to do all the things well which are expected or required of us. This is particularly true of those successful and gifted persons who by virtue of their proficiency and success are expected to take on even more responsibilities than others. Just talk to a successful government official or executive or to a conscientious homemaker and parent who has decided to launch a new career or academic program in mid-life. Parkinson's Law, which states that existing work expands to fill the available time for it, is accurate to an exaggerated degree for the proficient or gifted person in particular.

In addition, those who rely upon these gifted individuals—families, friends, bosses, employees, communities—expect more from them. The result is resentment directed toward the giver for not meeting all those expectations.

For much of my own life I have wanted to do far more things than I could do well. The result is that I am able to do many things, but not until the past ten years of my life have I really begun to focus on doing a few things well.

I have paid a price for not taking better care of myself. That price has been that, not only did I suffer from the frenetic life which I lived, but I had little left to give to others with whom I especially desired to share my life.

Often the talented person is tempted to say yes to every challenge, to every invitation to "perform," or to serve others. Learning to say no to such invitations is an important and necessary way to be tender toward yourself. Learning how to say no tenderly but firmly is difficult for many of us. But unless we nurture ourselves, we have little nurture left to share with others. Some people are afflicted with a neurotic desire to nurture the entire universe of needy people. It won't work for them or those they want to "help." Many of these people are obvious to spot, but they are not the ones I am concerned about. It's the less obvious "pleasers" who appear to do so many things well that I'm speaking to. (I know. I've been one myself.)

We frenetic achievers are often so torn and harassed that our emotions and bodies are closed off to others and our spirits are in hiding.

We need to learn to say *no* instead of yes to every proposal or request that comes to us. Saying no is a way of taking care of and being tender to yourself. You really don't (and can't) meet everyone else's expectations. Several years ago, I told myself, "Hal, take care of yourself; you don't have to meet everyone else's expectations."

Most of my life I have tried to meet others' expectations of how I should behave. I knocked myself out trying to make myself indispensable on the job. For some bosses I was the perfect assistant or deputy, with my intense desire to please and get the job done, even beyond what my bosses expected. In doing this, my family suffered and I suffered, but I was too numb to experience the pain. This certainly was not taking care of myself. It was taking care of the image I held of myself. I had accepted the conditioning that the human body can bear incredible pain and punishment and still survive.

I recall how hard I worked at running track and cross-country at West Point almost every day for four years. In the fall there was the grueling cross-country course in the hills above the academy; in the winter there was indoor track; and in the spring, outdoor track. I was never a star. I hardly ever won a race at West Point, where the intercollegiate competition was stiff, as I had in high school when I was co-captain of the team. Yet I was one of those regulars who would occasionally come in third or fourth—just enough to win my varsity letter and keep the stars on their toes by pushing them closer to their greater potential. However, the glory of the "thoroughbred" was theirs. I was a workhorse, and work I did—every day. I recall often forcing my body to the degree that it would protest by loudly dry-heaving all around the last quarter mile, but that wouldn't stop me. I would just pour it on harder. Coach Crowell would tell us to "lean into the pain," that the human body is capable of enduring far more than we could ever imagine. It became a "race of life" for me. (I even wrote a poem, "The Race of Life," which I gave to the coach.) I was certain that if I gave up psychologically on the third lap of the mile or on the last mile of the cross-country course, I would give up in everything in my life (which I viewed as a race against all the other competitors). Most of my life, until recently, I have been running this race. Some good has come of it. I want to retain my ability to *run*, which I'm sure will never be a problem for me, but I want to take better care of myself by not running needlessly—on the track, or in life.

The Israeli therapist Moshe Feldenkrais literally brought

David Ben-Gurion back to life through his body/mind integra-
tion work. Ben-Gurion used to run ten miles a day for several
years before his death in December 1973. Moshe Feldenkrais
has worked with Olympic athletes in just the opposite mode,
improving their performance many times by prescribing *re-
duced* workouts and elimination of all painful or forced training.

I also have begun to reject my own conditioned response
that pain equates with progress and virtue. I no longer jump
through everyone else's hoops. I take my vacation when I want
to, because I care enough about myself. I refuse to take my work
home or to work on weekends unless it is something I personally
want to do, because that time belongs to me and my family. If
I feel sick, instead of acting the stoic, as I always did in the
military, I am beginning to allow myself to have my sickness—
to feel it rather than to deny it. This has been difficult for me,
getting over my scornfulness toward those who were weak or
couldn't discipline themselves enough to finish the race or the
six A.M. five-mile runs on which I used to lead my paratrooper
company; or the so-called deadbeats who invariably joined the
sick-call ranks to escape military training, even among the elite
airborne paratroopers. When others were feeling sick or tired
or depressed, I had a problem not laying my scorn on them and
not allowing them—or myself—to feel sick. I am changing as I
learn to become tender toward myself.

The "you don't have to meet everyone else's expectations"
part of my personal mantra is still difficult for me. I have discovered that many of these expectations really are my own projec-
tions. I expect me to be fair, witty, bright, clever, successful,
entertaining, lovable, sexy, open-minded, fearless, and much
more.

I am still working to cultivate this self-honesty. When I am
tired, I am now beginning to admit it. I am not always sexy. I

am occasionally fearful. I am not always clever. Occasionally I am a bore. Certainly I am occasionally less than honest, and I am working hard on allowing myself to be unreasonable—but this is very difficult for someone as rational as I have been trained to be. I'm finding that it is mostly my own assumptions of what I think others expect that I try to meet, and I am working on giving this up.

I work at cultivating these seeds. They have sprouted, but they are slow-growing and need lots of tender care if they are to really bear substantial fruit in my life. Perhaps my old weeds are choking the new seedlings. Some of these I am pruning out. Others that were labeled "bad seed" I am beginning to accept and even love and appreciate. An inner voice reminds me, "A human being who has not a single hour for his own every day is no human being."

We give up so much of our life to society, to the rat race. We even give up our time with our families and loved ones for the sake of our demanding jobs. Don't we value ourselves enough to set aside time for ourselves? Don't I value myself enough? I'm in a struggle as I write: the old impasse between society and me, between environmental and self-support. There are so many convenient rationalizations for doing it society's way.

Rationalizations don't help us to take risks, by and large. They keep us stuck in our patterns of false "security." It's still my life. I've got to live it.

As I look back over the first thirty years of my life and the varied pursuits I've followed, it is as though I felt I had to fill my life—fill each day, fill each weekend—with spectacular achievements. I did this even when I was thinking or fearing that there was nothing spectacular within me, or between me and others. Many couples pack their entire weekends with a frenzy of activities when they suspect there is nothing spectacular between them as people. I remember planning extraordinary events for my family's time together so we could really enjoy the *events*. (Since probably we weren't really enjoying each other?)

A teacher who feels he or she has to fill the void—the void of having nothing in common with his or her students—is in the same bind. I fill my life with "extraordinary events" when I feel I have nothing within myself alone. Such events—the delicious meal that I cook, a party that I host—are not bad. In fact, they're fine, but they are supplementary. For many years I treated these activities as the main event, tuning out the people that I was in the presence of (not with) in preference to the busy work of the spectacular dramas I had learned only too well to stage.

Take a look at your life. Are you paying more attention to the activities or events than to the people in your life?

If so, you are not taking good care of yourself. You can be tender toward yourself by saying no to more of the activities and busy work and yes to more of the people you do them with —and, in particular, to yourself.

A Complex-Looking Machine Is Simple; a Simple-Looking Man Is Complex

Many men I know own sports cars. Some own them just for the fun of driving them around and feeling the tension of machinery in motion. Others own them for the peacock pleasure of being seen in them. And still others own them because they enjoy making all of the adjustments and tuning refinements which these cars require. Over the years, I have found it fascinating to watch this third group of sports-car enthusiasts. For these men, their cars are like enormous tinker-toys. They never stop fiddling with them. At one level it doesn't make any sense; these guys are such good mechanics that their cars are never really out of tune. So the work they do on them is really play. It's not done to make the cars work better. It's done to make their owners *feel* better. The car is just a toy to work on, a way of letting the owner feel good about himself as an amateur mechanic.

Many of us have such hobbies or interests in which we immerse ourselves. It's a beautiful relationship. These men— many of whom are tense, worried executives, others of whom labor long hours in factories—all find a way to relax with their steel and chrome companions. Our cars don't talk back or disagree with us. And when we work on them and make effective adjustments in their steering or carburetion, the cars respond in kind and provide us with an immediate feeling of satisfaction. In return for their careful work, car buffs are given years of faithful service from their mechanical "friends." It is almost touching to see how much care and concern robust men will devote to these mechanical objects.

Almost touching—and just a little frightening. As I watch these men polishing and tuning their cars I always stop to wonder if they devote the same care and concentration to other areas of their lives; and if I, with some of my intense interests, really devote enough attention to the hidden mechanisms of my own self. How many wives must wonder the same? And how many sons learn about cars just so they can spend some time with their fathers?

But what is most alarming about this strange love affair is that many of us who are engrossed in our hobbies seem to know far more about the inner workings of these amateur pursuits than we do about our own bodies and emotional interiors. It is nothing for us to spend long hours getting the right note out of our exhaust system or stripping down an engine to replace a gasket. Yet how many of us would even think of spending the same amount of time doing yoga or experimenting with our diets to see what results *these* kinds of fine-tuning adjustments will provide us? Many of us are overweight, undernourished, and sadly out of touch with ourselves. We can strip a car down, but we are afraid to spend any time alone with our own thoughts. We can find the trouble in a roaring engine, yet our own roaring minds are mysteries to us. When we suffer too much mental tension, we take our problem to a therapist and leave it up to him. When our bodies "act up," we visit our doctor and listen respectfully to his instructions as though he were telling us about some deep dark mystery. Yet, when we take our cars in to the dealer to have some work done on them, we worry and fret and hover over the shop mechanics as though they were performing surgery on an infant. It is preposterous, when you think about it. We are human beings who often know, and apparently care, more about machinery than about ourselves. And, for many American men, what I am describing is the norm, not the exception.

What is more, many of us who labor so long and so lovingly over cars would think it totally ridiculous to spend as much time or attention on ourselves. We are comfortable with cars, yet uncomfortable with ourselves. We consider it masculine and manly to devote the tenderest attentions to the intricacies of a V-8, yet the same degree of care applied to ourselves strikes us as a little suspicious.

And so we have reached the situation in America where a "successful" man may own two beautiful sports cars which he keeps in perfect condition, while he himself drops dead suddenly of a heart attack one day, "with no advance warning." All the warning he needed was there, in his own self-neglect. But he was too busy tuning his engines to listen to his own body. A machine, no matter how complicated-looking, is the most simple of *things.* A man, no matter how simple-looking, is the most complicated of *beings.*

This example of the sports-car *aficionado* is repeated in many other ways: we weekend athletes and Monday morning quarterbacks who can quote the latest statistics on our favorite team's players but who somehow forget how many calories we keep consuming; we do-it-yourself master builders who can finish off our basements but who cannot sit quietly in meditation in them; and we Don Juans who can pocket the hearts of our ladies but who somehow never understand our own emotions. All of us have one thing in common: we project our concern and tenderness *outward*—onto cars, basements, baseball teams, our buddies in bars, and the barmaids we may hope to take home. But we keep missing the target that is closest to home—ourselves. We can spend hours tenderly weeding and watering our gardens, but we will gulp down a meal that someone else has spent hours cooking for us. We are tender toward objects, gruff with people, oblivious to our own bodies, and afraid of our own emotions.

We are not "bad." We are perplexed. We do not realize how poorly proportioned our·lives are. We are tender toward our cars and gardens, and we do not see how tough we are on ourselves. And we are afraid to find out. We do not see that it is not a sign of weakness to let others come close to us, but a sign of welcome. We do not know this because no one has ever shown us. And whenever anyone tries, we tend to chase the unwelcome intruder off. We are so lost in our pictures of what a "real man" is, that we have lost sight of the fact that we human beings are, in one respect, just small animals without even any fur or sharp teeth to protect us. What protects us is not our viciousness but our humanity: our ability to love others, and to accept the love that others want to offer us. It is not our toughness that keeps us warm at night but our tenderness which makes others want to keep us warm.

Tenderness toward the self can be expressed in many ways. Some of us do this instinctively, by always taking the best possible care of our bodies, these incredible living machines we have been given to carry us through life, and by treating ourselves with dignity and respect, just as we would want anyone else to treat us.

On the other hand, at times we treat our bodies as naughty children or as nasty burdens we have to carry around through life. At times we display an attitude toward ourselves which is anything but tender. It is harsh, it is judgmental, it is often brutal.

When we do this, we make our bodies pay for the unhappiness in our hearts. But if we would look deeper into our hearts, we might find a deeper happiness which we could use to nourish ourselves no matter how the world treats us. The wheel of fortune is always spinning. Some days we win, some days we lose. We can always be winners if we treat ourselves, *our*selves, with the respect and tenderness we need and deserve. There are many ways to do this, if we are willing to learn.

Eating Tenderly

One way which many people are beginning to explore more seriously is the intelligent use of a natural diet. Diet is a perfect litmus test of how much in touch we are with ourselves. People who are constantly on the run, who are nervous, who are hard-nosed in their dealings with the world, also will be nervous, hard-nosed, and hurried in the way they treat themselves. They will treat their meals more like pit stops in a race than as moments to renew their strength and to nourish their spirits. Someone who gobbles a hamburger in ten seconds is only going to have to spend that much longer digesting what he has literally thrown down his throat. Our bodies are not gas tanks.

When we *are* out of touch, we will eat indiscriminately, basing our food choices more on sentiment and advertising than on any actual knowledge of food combinations or of what our body is telling us it needs when we take it out for lunch.

Even less likely are we to take any consideration of how our meals are prepared, whether with a spirit of attention or care, or whether they are simply slapped together like a beef patty between two balloon-sized buns. There is a natural foods restaurant in Washington, D.C., appropriately called "The Golden Temple," where I love to go to eat and where I enjoy taking my friends. It is run by yoga students, and the care and attention which these young people show toward their patrons by the way they prepare and serve their food is remarkable. It communicates a real feeling of warmth, caring, and peace. When I look around the restaurant at the other people eating there, I always notice that people are eating their meals slowly and are talking quietly, just as I find myself doing. There is something about the food which makes one slow down, pay attention to it, and treat it as an offering—not as a tankful of fuel to be poured into the body. We are not automobiles. We are people. Our bodies reflect the way we think and feel. Cars are polished from the outside. People are polished from within.

Although diet affects everyone, there seems to be a particular set of masculine attitudes and assumptions about food which dictate what a "man" is supposed to eat. Men, so goes this attitude, are supposed to eat meat-and-potatoes, and lots of it. "Meat-and-potatoes" sounds very substantial, and it is. That is the whole problem with it. It is a very heavy diet, hard for the body to break down into usable protein.

The cow may once have been running around, but eating beef tends to slow people down. Often the meat is so difficult to digest that it actually takes more energy from the body to digest a steak than the steak provides in return. But few men realize this. Most of us seem to eat our mental "pictures" of what a good meal is supposed to look like. We don't ask our bodies what they actually need.

If we did, we might find that our bodies can sustain themselves very well on a variety of very simple natural foods. Fruits, vegetables, brown rice, soybeans, sprouted seeds, salads, whole grains, yogurt, and kefir—all of these are foods which offer maximum *live* protein (as contrasted with the protein in meat, which already has been stripped of its life). There is another, more subtle difference in these foods. They are gentle toward the body. They do not sit like lead weights, slowly decomposing inside the stomach. They are quickly digested and assimilated into the body for use. The difference in time and energy between the body's ability to digest a light salad and a heavy steak can be as much as four or five *days*.

You can discover this for yourself. If you are a meat-and-potatoes man, simply notice how you feel after a large meal. Notice in particular how tight your stomach is. That tight, stuffed feeling is the result of cramming in too much food, food which is very difficult for your body to digest. What happens as a result is that the body can take as long as five days to process that one meal.

And in the meantime you have eaten fifteen other meals, many of them just as big. It is no wonder that so many of us men have distended stomachs. We are overfed and undernourished. And the irony is that many of us assume that by eating more we are eating better. We even pride ourselves on our ability to pack it away. The body is not a suitcase, however. It is also the person who must carry the suitcase. Americans, men in particular, consume far more in quantity and far less in quality than we need.

Continuing with our little experiment, in the following few weeks try eating a few meals which are very light and simple: a salad of fresh greens with sprouts and wheat germ sprinkled on top, perhaps with a dressing of soy sauce, lemon juice, and grated ginger; or yogurt and mixed fresh fruit with some sunflower seeds and honey mixed into it; or a fresh whole-grain cereal sweetened with natural maple syrup instead of sugar; or a loaf casserole of brown rice and soybeans (a perfect food combination, as these two foods when mixed produce a complete protein). If you are willing to try this simple experiment, then do it right, and give your body a chance by eating several of these light, natural meals successively. Don't just eat one meal and expect to be able to tell the difference. The effect of eating well is cumulative, so give the experiment at least two or three days to work. *Then* notice how you feel. I can almost guarantee that you will feel lighter, *more* energetic (since you won't be spending nearly as much energy on digestion), and less stuffed.

Unfortunately, many men view such a natural-foods diet as something that is all right for women or for small animals, but not for "men." Perhaps it is a carryover from our ancestry as hunters. But times and culture have changed drastically. Most of us do not hunt for our meals any more, and few of us even farm for them. That may be one reason why we accept so uncritically the processed, manufactured "foods" which our supermarkets display. But it is all the more reason for us to take our bodies' needs seriously and to treat them with love and respect. The alternative is the same built-in obsolescence that afflicts our automobiles: cars falling apart after three years, and people dying of heart attacks, completely without warning, at age forty-five. But the warnings were there every night, on the dinner table.

Whatever the male attitude about food may be, the fact is that all food energy is simply a form of converted sunlight. Cows don't eat steak. Cows eat grass. When we eat steak, *we* are eating grass. And what is grass but sunlight? Sunlight, the most basic form of energy. Grass, green vegetables, fruit, grains, even meat—all these foods are sunlight. There is no virtue in com-

plicating the structure of the food we eat. Meats are very complicated, and thus require a long time for the body to break
down. And at the end of the digestion process, all we can get
is—sunlight. Why not learn to create an efficient, nourishing
diet out of the *simplest* carriers of sunlight: live foods.

They are still glowing with light and life. When you eat these
foods, you can, after a while, literally feel the light and liveliness
of the food tingling in your body. Light is a powerful force, like
life itself. It is also a very subtle force, one that many of us tend
to overlook, especially if we are focused on male images of what
"a man's meal" ought to be.

There is a great difference between just filling the body up
at a hamburger drive-in, or overstuffing it at a restaurant feast,
and actually nourishing it with tender, wholesome, and simple
meals which are tailored to the body's true needs. Try the
experiment of feeding yourself tenderly, chewing your food
thoroughly until it is completely liquefied in your mouth, and
eating three days of natural, live foods. Then see how you feel.
I think you will find that by treating yourself tenderly and with
respect, you will experience more alertness and more energy.
Tenderness is *not* weakness. It is the path to greater strength.

I have developed a practice of engaging in periodic "fasts"
for three to six days. During these periods, I do not starve myself
but rather eat a simple diet of a cup of cooked brown rice three
times a day, followed in half an hour by a cup of sassafras tea.
I find that it is not always practical to eat my healthy "ideal" diet
while living and working with others in the establishment, particularly at conferences, in social settings, or on other such occasions.

People are important to me and getting together to share
food is a traditional way to be with people. So I find myself often
eating foods which are not always the best or tenderest for my
body. At other times I just plain enjoy eating a steak, a venison
roast, or a wild goose.

A periodic cleaning out of my body through a fast helps tune me up. The brown rice not only provides needed protein, but it acts as a plug of roughage to literally sweep out the intestinal tract. The sassafras tea should be drunk without sugar or sweetener half an hour after eating the rice so as not to dilute the stomach acids which are working on the rice fiber. Sassafras tea is a wonderful solvent, helping to dissolve the residue of old pills, drugs like aspirin, or antibiotics or other toxic matter which tends to collect in the mucous membranes of the intestines. About the third day of such a fast, I find my senses beginning to sharpen up (particularly my sense of smell of other tempting foods). After the hurdle of the third day, it gets easy to continue on for two or three more days. From the fourth day on, I find an incredible increase in consciousness. My mental capacity and creativity seem to be dynamically enhanced. I am literally "high" in awareness. Even my ability to anticipate—my "precognition" or ESP ability—seems to become available to me. All of my senses are sharpened and a special bonus is that I usually lose five to ten pounds of accumulated excess pouch weight in a five- or six-day fast. Plus my complexion clears and softens as the toxins gradually leave the skin.

At these times when I fast, I feel a peaceful kind of tenderness pervading my being which is difficult to describe. Meditation in combination with the fasting is especially poignant for me. I recommend that before launching on such a fast you get your physician's O.K. just to insure that you have no ailments that would be complicated by the fast (in fact, you might even cure some). None of these practices are new, except to some of us from the Western culture. But then we Westerners are beginning to learn a great deal from Eastern cultures about our inner selves. We have been so busy in this pioneering country of America, conquering new outer frontiers through our toughness, that it is high time for us to explore our inner frontiers through softer and more tender approaches.

Meditation As a Means to Tenderness

Another Eastern practice that helps me to treat myself with tenderness and respect is the practice of meditation. Though I had experienced much therapy and most of the recent developments in the human potential movement, I had never meditated until recently. I now find that as little as thirty minutes per day spent in quiet meditation can make my entire day creative, successful, and fulfilling. It is an easy way to tap my own deep inner strength and my reserves of love and bliss—energies which are hidden within us all.

Meditation provides for me what prayer provides for some people. I've always been a fast-moving, double-energy-level person with ten or fifteen projects on the burner all at once. Through the process of meditation I find I can slow down to a peaceful state and find within myself an increased capacity for love, spiritual strength, and tenderness. Just as aluminum and copper are excellent conductors of electricity, while lead isn't a conductor at all, tenderness is an excellent conductor for love.

A person who is tender is an excellent conductor of love to other people. When I go inside myself through the meditation process, I find myself filled with feelings of incredible love, beauty, and bliss. When I finish, I find myself in a very peaceful, relaxed state. I usually meditate for thirty minutes in the morning, after I do some physical exercise. Usually I take a one-mile run, shower, and then I sit in an upright position with my hands in an open posture in a darkened room. I feel as though I'm "receiving" myself, and I just try to focus on nothingness. I say a mantra that I learned from a very high being, Swami Muktananda. This mantra, which I chant over and over, literally means, "I worship my own inner self."

This "self" is in all of us, waiting to be released. Yet we are so busy with our external affairs that we ignore and neglect our own inner strength. In essence, it is a form of tenderly falling in love with yourself. Not until you love yourself will you have the real capacity to connect with the love within others. It's as though there's a radio channel of love all around us, but our transmitters and receivers are tuned to other channels and numb to love. By going within and connecting with our own inner bliss and love, we automatically turn on our channel to all others who have theirs turned on to all the beauty and natural love in nature (which is always "turned on"), and we are literally connected to and in love with the world.

So tenderness toward the self—caring for yourself—is a vital first step, perhaps the most important step in realizing that tenderness is strength, your own inner strength which can then become available for you to share with others. There are many ways of being tender to ourselves. No matter how hard we pursue it, we will never get all the tenderness we desire from others, or from any external sources. Yet within each of us there exists this well of boundless love and tenderness.

The mantra helps me to sweep out my thoughts, like old cobwebs out of the corners of a room. Sometimes I see visual imagery of different light spots and lines, and I just let my attention flow with them when I see them. And then I finally reach this special place of "nothingness" (which I'm never able to do for my entire meditation, since my mind is racing and I'm going back again through the mantra to where I started from).

But every once in a while I'll get into a place where I start beaming from within. A smile will spread across my face, and that's an outward sign to me that I've reached a peaceful place, where my own inner strength and tenderness really begin—the source of it all. I'll try to stay there, but my mind is such a devil it goes everywhere else, and I'll try to turn it off and go back to "source." The longer I stay in that nothingness state, the longer the meditation seems to last with me. After the meditation I often find that people will look at me and say, "Hey, what's happened to you?" They detect a transformation all over my being. I think it takes the lines out of my face and the tension out of my body, my mind, and my emotions. This is a very good way for me to get in touch with my tenderness. I become "centered." I am no longer worried about everyone else's evaluation or approval of me. I feel myself getting that from within myself. I am no longer responding; I am just being.

During my adolescent years I was quite religious, looking to God for answers and trusting that if I earned His approval, He would take care of and look after me and my needs. Then came a period of years—West Point, the military, government—when I sought to earn the approval of other mortals, people like myself who, if I pleased them, would in turn take care of, reward, and nurture me.

More recently I have grown to the place where I now have what might be called a "religion of the self." I believe that most of the answers are within myself and that learning to tap the love and beauty and strength within myself is really a worshiping of the inner self. In essence, I believe in God. God is within each of us. We are all God and, hence, all one. For a Buddhist or a Taoist the goal for living is to embrace the entire world within one's ego boundaries—and thus reach a union with all others. I am neither a Buddhist nor a Taoist, but just as I used to pray to an external God, I now meditate to the God within my own inner self; and each time I meditate, I discover new resources of boundless love and beauty within myself. I believe that we all share this same inner source of strength.

est: To Be Tender, Learn to Just Be

Over a hundred thousand people in this country have been through the est training. *Est* is Latin for "it is." Many est "graduates," including myself, have gotten considerable value out of this intensive sixty-hour training. Though there has been some controversy about the est training, stirred mainly by people who have not experienced it, I feel this synthesis of many Eastern philosophies and human potential practices provides an excellent vehicle for our becoming more in touch with and tender toward ourselves and others. One of the est principles is that we are perfect just the way we are. "What is, is. What's so, is so—so what?"

There is a subtle yet important difference between this attitude and fatalism. The fatalistic person just leaves everything to fate. For this person, "what will be, will be." Fatalism is more a surrender to the future. Yet the truth is that our energies *now* can change what the future will be. It is the *now* that we cannot change. Hence, "what *is,* is." This is difficult to understand and it takes most of the sixty hours of est for the trainees to get it. But in essence, if you choose the present to be what it is, you always win, because you choose what *is.* If you fret over the present instead of choosing it, you spin your wheels wasting needless energy.

If your present or "now" is miserable, and you fret about it, you lose. If instead you choose it (make a conscious choice that what is, is), the misery has an uncanny way of disappearing. You are not choosing misery, you are really choosing that misery is what is *now.* And that leads to misery not being what is, a moment later. So one very real way to be tender toward yourself is to choose your *now* rather than to hate it, because what is, is. This leads to a greater trusting of the here-and-now eternal "source" within us that is our "guide," which leads to a personal transformation of our way of being in life: our life works. When I'm in touch with that "guide," I become less upset with any part of me that may not be working right or isn't living up to my own expectations. Most of us tend to have very high expectations for ourselves.

Since I also judge myself by my own high standards, *and* by other people's standards, by showing tenderness toward myself through trusting this inner "guide," I allow myself to be guided rather than driven, and I do not worry too much about what I am doing. People who are toughest are usually tougher on themselves than on anyone else. The people who drive other people often drive themselves even harder. Being tender toward yourself, looking inward, treating yourself well, will also lead to your taking better care of others. One of the signs that someone is really growing is that he begins to take it easy on himself and take better care of his life. Worry is not care. It is worry.

An Exercise for Tenderness Toward the Self

I'd like to introduce a short exercise I learned from Sid Simon, and his *Values Clarification* work, that I suggest you do at this time. Read the instructions, then put the book down and do the exercise. You'll need a piece of paper and a pencil. First write the numbers 1 through 20 down the left margin of the paper. Next, think of the twenty things you most like to do in your life. When you are being tender toward yourself, you'll naturally be putting into your life the things you like to do most. If you come up with more than twenty, narrow it down to twenty, and list those things on your paper in any order. Put short phrases such as "making love, eating a gourmet meal with a special person, playing tennis, going out to a movie," etc.

Next step, put a dollar sign after the things that cost over five dollars. You might be surprised to find that many of the things you like to do most in life don't cost much.

Next step, put a code letter after each item as follows: "A" if you like to do it *a*lone, "P" if you like to do it with other *p*eople, "S" if you like to do it with a *s*pecial person. This will tell you whether you're a loner and require a lot of space to do things by yourself and need to provide for that. This may mean, if you're married or in a relationship with someone, you'll need to negotiate to give yourself that kind of space. If you see that you like to do things with other people, you might want to increase your social life. If you like to do them with special people, and you don't have those kinds of relationships, perhaps you ought to begin looking for that kind of special person to do your favorite things with.

Next step, put a big "R" after each item that is a high risk for you. If you find you have a lot of high-risk things, maybe you ought to start risking doing some of those things, and you'll find that the risks may start to disappear as they become easier for you, and as you treat yourself better by doing those things.

Next step, put a number 5 after each item that would not have been on your list five years *ago*. This will tell you whether or not you are changing. Also put a number 10 by each item you do not expect to be there ten years from *now*. This will tell you that this is a temporary value.

Next step, put a little heart symbol by each item you feel you would want to have your special people put on their lists. Later, introduce this exercise to these special people. Don't tell them what you have on your list. After they do the exercise, sit down together and see how many compatible items you have. If there are five things on both your lists, here are five things that you can enjoy together. The other fifteen on your list are important to you, and you need to do them if you are to be tender toward yourself. So you may have to negotiate some space for them. Maybe one of yours would have been twenty-first on the other person's list, so he'd like to do it with you anyway. Or maybe you'd like to do it with someone else. If you like the opera and your special person doesn't, then maybe you have to negotiate space for you to go to the opera with some other friend. And sometimes that can be difficult. But remember, these twenty things are important to you. Date your list, file it away and do the exercise again a year later and see if it's the same. Do it five years later. This is a good exercise to determine how seriously you take your own desires, and how tender you are toward yourself in satisfying them.

Recognize that being tender with yourself is to *experience* satisfaction from within, instead of thinking that what you want in life exists outside you.

Many people like to eat oranges. Other people don't. When someone really tastes an orange and it's so sweet and juicy and good, and another person eats it and doesn't like it at all, there is nothing different about the orange. It's some different inner quality about the people that causes one to enjoy it more. There is some inner quality in human beings that creates the capacity to experience satisfaction. But it is interesting that all of us have the "source" of satisfaction within ourselves.

So one way to increase your satisfaction with yourself and increase your tenderness toward yourself is to realize that the satisfaction that we all seek in life is within us. It is not something that lies outside us. Even with the people we love most, the ones we think we could never do without, it's something in *us* that responds to them. They put us in touch with something invaluable in ourselves, so we find them valuable. Even with your best friend, it's something in *you* that you enjoy feeling when you are in the presence of that other person. That something you enjoy feeling is within you. So when you realize this satisfaction and joy is "sourced" right within your own self, then you don't have to feel so upset with yourself when you are not with your favorite people or are not doing one of your favorite twenty things.

Whatever you are doing, you can stop your world for a moment. Close your eyes. Bring that feeling of satisfaction and well-being from within you back up to the surface of your awareness.

Realize that it is right there inside you all the time, waiting. You may think that you can only feel it when you are doing one of those twenty things on your list, but the fact is you can feel it any time. However, our minds are usually not geared to let us experience this. We live in a culture where items are sold to us because they "make" us feel good. Ultra-Brite toothpaste is good because it will "make" us sexy and happy. Happiness is treated as sort of a commodity, because that's the way the advertising people know they can sell products. You know the best things in life really are free and they come from right within you. You don't have to get them from anyone else.

Asking for What You Want

Since one way to express tenderness toward yourself is to put in your life more of the things you'd like, you can begin to ask for those things. The healthy person is willing to risk asking for what he wants. The person who asks gets what he wants a lot more often than the person who sits back waiting, hoping that someone will give it to him, or hoping that chance will bring it his way. Yet, learning to ask is risky, because you can be turned down. But asking is a way to be clear. Asking is also a skill. Making a statement does not make you as vulnerable as asking a question does. And it is easy for a person not to be clear in his response to a statement because *statements* are sometimes not as clear as questions.

The beautiful thing about specific questions is that people usually have to respond clearly to them, whereas statements do not require that. Sometimes people think they are asking questions when they are really making statements. If you make the statement to a woman "I wish you'd visit me," and her response is "I'd like to," you have not been altogether clear and neither has she. She hasn't really expressed whether she wants to visit you or not. And you haven't really been clear about your desire.

If you ask, "Will you come to see me tomorrow?" it becomes much more explicit, because she now has to answer either yes or no. And then you know clearly where she stands, and so does she. You can then decide what you are going to do. So you get clarity from her through the question. But you are also vulnerable, and that vulnerability leads to intimacy. It's a very tender thing to ask the question; and if you ask questions you are likely to get more of what you want, which is one way of being tender to yourself and caring about yourself.

Celebrating the Little Boy or the Little Girl in You

As I walk through the first-class section of an airplane or sit in the waiting room for a flight and observe the impatient, stone-faced executives, I wonder what happened to the tender little boy in each of them. I am shocked every time I realize that perhaps I am one of them and that this might be happening to me.

This same question comes to mind in government meetings, board rooms, and business offices wherever I go. What happened to the playful little boy and little girl in each of us?

The sad answer is that it was scared away or killed off by the seriousness of adults, parents, teachers, bosses, boards of education, institutions, governing bodies, and many others in positions of authority to evaluate the behavior of us all. Do we fit? Do we measure up to adult standards? Have we adopted adult standards for ourselves? There is very little room in such competitive seriousness for the little boy or girl in each of us. It's no wonder that we are overjoyed (if we are open-minded and free enough), or offended and threatened (if we are strait-laced) by the rare individual who is able to own both the adult *and* the child within him- or herself. This is the tender, spontaneous, playful, fun-loving part of us that it is a joy to be with, which lies dormant and often oppressed beneath our tough, serious exteriors.

Take a look in the mirror at yourself sometime. Where is the little boy or girl in you? He or she is in there hiding. How long has it been since you let him or her out to play? When was the last time you looked in the mirror and made a funny or grotesque face at yourself? If you can't remember, you may be taking yourself and life too seriously. See yourself the next time you look in the mirror.

If your little boy or girl is close under the surface just yearning to get out, this little act of personal rebellion might help him or her venture out to play. If he or she is too deeply buried beneath your toughness, it will take more therapeutic growth to free your tender little boy or girl parts.

Tenderness toward ourselves is such an important step in improving our ability to express tenderness toward others. It is within us all to be tender to others, and it all begins within ourselves. Tenderness toward the self is the beginning of true strength.

7 The Courage to Fear

As an impressionable young man I was conditioned to value courage as the manly trait above all others. I am only now beginning to discover that it also takes courage to be fearful.

Ordinarily, we numb ourselves to avoid fear. The body automatically prepares itself for threatening situations. Adrenaline pumps into the bloodstream, enabling us to flee, fight, or endure the pain of possible injury. The body tenses, and breathing becomes shallow and restricted. Our body armor bristles, and we become numb to almost anything. This response occurs in varying degrees whether the threat is emotional or physical.

Such a response is most appropriate in a survival situation, in combat, or in the jungle—whether in the Congo or in concrete. But with other human beings for whom we care, such a defensive posture only insures our isolation and guarantees us against intimacy.

Fools: Free of Fear—Wise Men: Free to Be Fearful

The macho male never admits that he is afraid. In our society, to admit that you fear is to admit that you are weak. Yet he who does not experience fear is either numb, or a fool, or both. It is only a fool who thinks he is free of fear. The wise man is free to feel fear. He is wise enough to accept that at times he *is* afraid. But he is also free of being fearful. He does not live *in* fear; he simply knows that there are times when he feels it. It takes strength and courage to admit that you are afraid. Once again, such an admission is a vulnerable act and the act of owning up to your fear can bring you into closer contact with others whom you love, and with yourself.

I recall from high school days our football coach telling the linemen just before a game that the first play from scrimmage would be the most important—that it could set the stage for the entire game, and that it was essential for us to get the psychological advantage over the players lined up opposite us by letting them know beyond a doubt that we were tougher. He suggested that this first play of the game was the time to be courageous, to put every ounce of energy into that charge, to growl, and hit the opponent in the face with your forearm as hard as you could during that charge to put fear into him. He maintained that from then on throughout the rest of the game we could keep the upper hand both psychologically and physically. This is the kind of macho toughening that many men are subjected to when young and that we carry over into other parts of our lives. "Never display fear. Make the other person fearful instead, so you can master him." It's no wonder that our tenderness hides within us after such early toughening.

The military provided postgraduate work in this, for all those who had that "privilege to serve." Those of us who did will remember bayonet training, where we were psychologically prepared with "the spirit of the bayonet" by screaming over and over, "Kill! Kill! Kill!" And then after the adrenaline was pumping, we raced through the course tearing, stabbing, and slashing at stuffed dummies (like dummies), all the time growling and yelling, "Kill!"

The Grand Deception: "I Am Not Afraid"

The truth is that we are all afraid, deep down beneath the tough shells and fronts we put up in order to convince all our other fearful comrades that we are not afraid. This is the grand deception. We are *all* cowards, *until* we admit that we are afraid. Our admission is our liberation.

I'm not speaking of the athletic field or the military in particular. I'm speaking of everyday situations between human beings, at the office, in bed, in the home, or in school. Disarming ourselves by having the courage to admit and share our fears will help those others, who are often also afraid to disarm themselves as well, rather than taking on the offensive posture of "Clobber them before they clobber us!"

Our fears go back to infancy, when we first feared being dropped, or being pulled away from mother's breast, or being put away in a dark room all alone, or awakening and not finding our parents there when we needed them. We would have had to be in a utopian environment to avoid such fears. We all have had them. Though we should all do the best we can to minimize these experiences for our children, we are not and cannot be perfect parents no matter how conscientious we are. Our adult fears frequently go all the way back to our own early childhood experiences of fear. Inevitably we tend to pass these on.

Our own therapeutic growth processes can help us uncover some of the pain we were too fearful and protected to experience as infants, which would have devastated us had we not blocked or numbed it in such tender times. Acknowledging our fears now is a step toward regaining our tenderness—the tenderness we all possessed as children, before we toughened ourselves to avoid the inevitable pain of survival in this often alienated and overly competitive society. And yet it involves a real risk to reveal to others that we are afraid, thus it is an act of courage rather than cowardice.

Intellectual Courage, Emotional Cowardice

Although I generally have been courageous in intellectual and physical matters, in emotional matters I find that I have been quite cowardly. I have had many emotional fears, and refusing to *admit* that I was afraid has compounded my cowardice. It takes some courage to admit that I am afraid. And, yes, I am afraid at times of rejection by a loved one, of not being accepted, of my own aloneness (though I have lately come to value this experience a great deal), and of death. When Leonard Cohen sings the song "Please Don't Pass Me By," he tells his audience that though they may not feel tonight or tomorrow that they need to know this song, sooner or later they will all "get down on their knees" in their old age, in sickness, or in rejection, and be vulnerable enough to ask someone not to pass them by. It takes courage for me to risk admitting that I am emotionally afraid.

But once I admit my emotional fear, then I am free of its stultifying, deceiving effects. Then I can face that fear squarely and deal with it, rather than deceiving myself and others by avoiding or burying it.

It is interesting how, when I give up taking responsibility for myself and my growth, disastrous results often emerge. I received a powerful lesson about this when I was twelve years old. I was such a "good boy" that I rarely tried to get out of going to school. However, one day a tough group of boys had threatened to beat me up, but as a result of my fleet-footedness I managed to evade them that afternoon after school. I was afraid to go to school the next morning; but rather than telling the real reason to my mother, I told her that I felt sick and had a sto-

machache. Since I rarely feigned illness, she readily consented
to my missing school. She asked where my stomach ached, and
I pointed to my right side. Her immediate reply was that it
could be my appendix, and with that she whisked me off to the
Army hospital, overruling my strong protests. Still not being
willing to take responsibility for my real reasons for staying
home, I was submitted to a battery of painful tests. The doctor
told my mother that it wasn't conclusive that I had appendicitis,
but that just to be sure he felt it was best to go ahead and
remove my appendix. This he did—all because of my unwilling-
ness to open my real fear! This tribulation was enough to decon-
dition me from ever feigning illness again, but not enough to
make me learn to take responsibility for my actions, or open
myself and my fears. That I am only beginning to learn now.

Do the Thing You Fear

I recall how in my high school days I read an old *Reader's
Digest* article with the title of "Do the Thing You Fear." At that
time I had a terrifying fear of speaking before an audience. I
decided I had to take the risk of doing this thing I feared, so I
volunteered to be master of ceremonies at the annual election
of cheerleaders assembly, held before the entire high school
student body. When I shared just the surface of my deep fear
with a friend, he suggested that I start off by telling a joke, a
process he maintained would relax my tension and the audience's as well. After listening around for appropriate jokes, I
finally settled on a rather elaborate one I felt would go over
well. As I stepped to the microphone (after checking repeatedly
to insure that my fly was not unzipped) I launched into my joke
with all the enthusiasm of a *Reader's Digest* hard sell.

About two-thirds of the way through the joke, I froze numb
with fear. I had listened to so many jokes by then that I was not

sure of the punch line. I hesitated and stared at the stony faces of the other students, while the punch line remained blocked in my mind.

In the front row my friend began to squirm uncomfortably, and then someone broke the silence with a giggle. Others joined in until the entire student body was laughing and applauding as my face flushed through several shades of red. Somehow, I began to laugh at myself, too. By accident, I had become vulnerable with them, and rather than clobbering me, somehow we had all become closer. I went on with the process of the cheerleader elections, empathizing with the girls now, and realizing that they, the cheerleaders, were at least as afraid as I had been. My goof made the cheerleaders less afraid of the mistakes that they might make. As I became more relaxed, I became more witty and natural, and I even began to enjoy the ceremony and my part in it.

The most attractive part of us is often the natural part that errs. Imperfection is a human trait. The perfect person is a straw man, a target for others to shoot down, proving to all that none of us is perfect. Our beauty is mixed with imperfections. When we try to have all the answers, we are role-playing, and though it may impress some, others will want to get beneath that veneer to find our imperfections, the human stuff in us all.

But *Reader's Digest* was right for me: "Do the thing you fear." It has worked many times since. However, I was a long time discovering that, though I had physical and intellectual courage, I also felt emotional cowardice. Admitting when I am emotionally afraid is a tender, vulnerable step toward closeness with others with whom I share life and life's fears. Admissions such as this make tenderness more possible for us.

While in Alaska a year ago, I watched in awe as the spawning salmon repeatedly catapulted themselves up against the cascades of a beautiful river with their mates to their spawning grounds. Where does this natural courage come from? Or what of the courage of the male praying mantis, who while copulating with his mate is triggered into the throes of orgasm by the act of her biting off his head and devouring him! We are all cowards compared to such freedom from being fearful. I am beginning to own many of my fears tenderly and becoming closer to others while doing so.

The courage to *be* with our fears is a real courage. Often it is harder than simple physical courage. By admitting to ourselves and to others that we are afraid, we take a necessary giant step toward freeing ourselves, and freeing them. It is the macho, the "tough guy," who cannot admit his fears, who insists on making a show of his "courage." The path toward tenderness often brings us to moments of doubt and fear. By softening our macho attitudes, we allow ourselves to feel our fear and to let it go. Then we are also free to experience our other feelings— and free to share these. The courage to fear also opens us to the freedom to feel.

8 The Tender Relationship

Tenderness is something we can experience in our relationships with others, as well as in our relationship to ourselves.

Many people act as though tenderness were a put-on sort of quality, like an emotional cosmetic. The typical cocktail party conversation is rife with cosmetic tenderness. Such dialogue may be genuine or may be phony. But if that is as far as the "tenderness" goes, it is superficial at best, and probably a seduction of some sort.

To be tender with another person means, first, being willing to experience a situation from the other person's point of view. In one of the novels of his *Alexandria Quartet,* Lawrence Durrell observes that life is far more complicated than any of us can possibly imagine, yet far simpler than we dare to suspect. Situations between people—relationships—are both simple and complex. The "tangled webs we weave" are often incredibly complex—so complex that we frequently need marriage counselors and psychologists to help us figure them out and untangle ourselves from them. Yet, at heart, a relationship is often also very simple: a strong emotional bond that develops naturally between people and which is so simple it does not need words to be expressed.

Unfortunately, many of us often adopt the position that the way we see reality is the way reality *is*. This is an error. The way we see things is only the way they are for *us*. Others see things differently and experience a different or a separate reality. By communicating our experience to one another, we come to share our lives and to expand the boundaries of our understanding as we learn to comprehend the experience and perspectives of others. This is how a child absorbs its picture of the world from its parents, teachers, and friends. And this is also how, as adults, we spread our leaves in the sun of humanity to gather warmth from one another.

But we can do this successfully only if we are willing, even temporarily, to adopt the points of view of other people. If we are always stuck in our own positions, we are like those old German rockets that trajected several hundred miles—but only in one direction, with no change possible. Yet consciousness is very mobile. We can be fixing dinner one minute, changing a diaper the next, helping a child with her homework after that, suddenly recalling things that happened many years ago, and then musing in wonder at the slow circling of the night sky. Human awareness is a precious and awesome instrument. We often take it for granted and fail to exercise it to anything near its potential.

One of the most amazing uses of human awareness is the ability to enter the experience of another consciousness. We can do this in many ways.

I mentioned earlier that recently I have begun to meditate and I find that meditation is a powerful tool for calming and centering my awareness. I like to meditate in many places, even when I am out in the woods early in the morning hunting.

Being in the woods is a special environment for me. I often

sit up in a tree and blend with nature. For me this becomes a meditation in itself. For years before I began meditating, I would at times listen for the animals and experience a feeling of becoming one with them. I would feel myself become the wild geese flying overhead, the squirrels, the owl hooting its "go ahead" signal at daybreak, and the deer moving mystically through the forest like a phantom. These animals become part of me, and in some way I also become part of them.

In a similar way we can also experience entering the consciousness of another person. This can occur in fleeting instants, as when we pick up the mental signals of others, often of people we don't know. People who know each other well can do this frequently. I am sure we have all known couples or brothers and sisters who frequently seem to know each other's feelings. Athletes who are teammates often report that during the intensity of a game they will somehow sense what the next moves of the partner will be, and they experience the game being played through them by intuition rather than by anything they "do." It just happens, and they are open enough to let it happen. The wisdom of intuition is often far quicker and more subtle than any conscious plans we can set. The more we can surrender to the moment and participate in it, the more aliveness we will experience. Life is simple. It is we who insist on making it complex.

In a long-term relationship, this ability to adopt the point of view or the feelings of the other person becomes extremely important. Relationships in which each party maintains his or her complete "independence" often do not develop in intimacy, but only in the mutually exclusive individuality of the two members. They become like billiard balls: shiny and hard on the outside, but never penetrating each other to go beyond the surface encounter. In such a relationship each person is focused not on what is shared but on what is private to himself.

As long as this focus is maintained, the relationship will remain stuck in this mutual selfishness. The two people may find that they need each other a great deal, but they will not be able to satisfy that need. They may experience growing frustrations about this. They may not see that they are being pulled in opposite directions because on the one hand they are adamant about their independence, while on the other hand they struggle to draw strength from each other.

Independence and Interdependence

Nourishing relationships are centered not so much on independence as on interdependence. One doesn't need a relationship to be independent. By definition, independence means not having to depend on anyone or any relationship. But there is a difference also between being independent and being individualistic. Someone who is individualistic seems to be always going it alone, whereas people who are independent draw strength from within themselves and are not afraid to enter into relationships with other strong people and thereby become interdependent. What happens when two strong people create a relationship?

Often at the outset what happens is a clash of wills, a kind of mutual testing of limits. If the two people are truly strong, they will be able to surrender their need to win, and will take their relationship to a new and more inclusive space where *both* can participate as equals *and* as winners. People who are constantly bickering and sniping at each other are displaying not strength but insecurity. They are saying that they cannot stand to be anywhere but on top, even for a moment. Their limits must be the other's limits.

There is also a difference between strength and stubbornness. Stubbornness is fixed, whereas strength flows. People who are truly strong are able to flow toward each other, rather than at each other. They can mix and merge their strengths, and they can open up spaces for each other to grow into and for the relationship as a whole to expand into. The ability to do this requires a prior willingness to move beyond one's position and to expand one's own ego boundaries.

There is an easy way to find out about how willing you are to give up a position in order to see things from someone else's point of view. The next time you and your partner are about to have an argument, see if you can look into her or his eyes, all the way past the particular issue that is dividing the two of you at the moment. See if you can make contact with that inner part of the other person which is just like the inner part of you: beautiful, pure, and strong. See if you can concentrate your awareness on that part of the other person. It shouldn't be hard, since you already know each other. Let your strength and caring flow out into the other person's eyes. Then see what happens.

Laughing Your Arguments Away

What often happens is that both people suddenly begin to laugh. Suddenly everything they were arguing about seems ridiculous and petty. They are able to see past their temporary disagreement and realize that what unites them is far more lasting and substantial than what is dividing their energies at that moment. So they laugh. And suddenly their argument changes character and becomes a shared joke on themselves. Suddenly they can see the argument for what it is: a blocked place in their continuing flow toward each other. Suddenly their argument becomes a veil to see through and to draw aside, rather than a wall between them. And through the medium of the argument itself they can realize that they are united and that this disagreement is a temporary barrier to experiencing that feeling of unity and at-oneness.

This ability to "get off it" and to transform disagreements into sources of mutual harmony and even laughter is not a uniquely human ability. Other animals also seem to do something similar to this. They stake out territories and attack any animal who ventures into them, and they have clearly defined senses of friend and foe. However, some animals possess an instinctive wisdom about fighting that we humans can learn from. Konrad Lorenz reports that when two wolves are fighting, and one wolf senses that it will be killed if it continues, it will suddenly make itself vulnerable by openly displaying one of its weakest parts, such as the underside of its belly or neck. This is a clear signal to its antagonist that it has had enough, and the adversary wolf will retreat and leave it alone, respecting its vulnerability rather than fighting on and killing it. We human beings could learn from this practice rather than "killing" a rival we have made vulnerable. However, as J. Bronowski stated in *The Ascent of Man*, "there must be something unique about man, because otherwise the geese would be lecturing about Konrad Lorenz and the rats would be writing papers about B. F. Skinner."

What we are able to do if we do "get off it" is to transform enemies into allies by the way we transform our viewpoint. In a tender and nourishing relationship, both partners will be able to transform their points of view to include the other person's experience—even if it is not one they would have chosen for themselves just then.

The ability to make this transformation of awareness is a hallmark of tenderness. A rigid person will not easily make such a transformation. A man attached to his position of being "right," as a know-it-all macho, for example, will feel threatened, not nourished, by the process of transformation I am describing. He will not see it as an opportunity to grow, but as a battle to be won—and thus he will keep his relationship at its previous level. He will not give his partner any space, nor will he give himself any. There is little growth space in having to be right all the time.

Tenderness, far from being a sign of weakness, is a touchstone of transformation and the gateway to it. Toughness, on the other hand, is a symptom of stagnation, of having to pay more and more to stay the same.

Who wants to stay the same? The point of being in relationships is to grow, to use the energies that each person brings to the relationship to create a new experience for both people. Meals are not cooked with just one food. Relationships are no different. The tender relationship makes full use of the inherent potentials for change and transformation which all of us possess, and it releases these by creating the space for them to be expressed and experienced.

One Plus One Equals Three: You, the Relationship, and Me

Relationships between two human beings are really three-part relationships instead of dualities. It's not just you and me that have to be nurtured. In addition to the "me" and the "you" there is the "us"—the relationship itself, which is like a third party. The "us" exists and it also requires special attention and care.

It's important that I take care of myself if I am going to have a good relationship with you. That's first. And it's important that you take care of yourself, because to the degree that we each love ourselves, and have worked out our own barriers to our own growth, we have that much more to share with each other. But the "us" also requires special maintenance. Unfortunately, many couples overlook the "us." But relationships don't just happen. They require work in maintaining their vitality. And that means sitting down periodically and actually working on the relationship by discussing candidly the barriers you feel are keeping you outside your own relationship. Few relationships exist without such barriers.

Most new devices that we purchase don't need as much upkeep initially as they do when they begin to get older. They do require maintenance if they are going to last for a lifetime, however, and relationships are certainly no different. New ones don't seem to need much maintenance. But if they are to be lifetime relationships, maintenance—the sharing of goals, strengths, barriers, and fears—must occur regularly. Then one plus one will equal three: you, the relationship, and me.

Relating Versus Co-existing

It is easy not to have hassles in your relationship if you skip shallowly across the surface of life rather than living deeply within it. You can quite easily "co-exist" with another person if you are not really intimate, if you don't take risks. But to live deeply means you are going to have peak highs and also rock-bottom lows.

Visualize a plane out in space. Let's say that your life hovers near that plane. If you just live life shallowly right next to the plane, or a bit above it and a bit below it, life will be quite hassle-free—but also quite boring. Picture a graph on that plane going up and down, piercing the plane at times, rising up into "living." All the space above the line is living, while below it is existing. To maximize our living, we need to go up as high as we can, spending as much time above the plane as we can. But, if we go up high, we'll also at times go plunging down through the plane from our heights to new depths. Instead of our life being represented by a flat, timid line, barely going up or down, the graph of a person who is taking the risks to live life deeply goes both up and down dynamically.

The tender relationship is one in which openness is prized. It's a relationship in which both partners take the risks of living deeply; but it is not one that is risk-free. Far from it. When both partners take risks, the tenderness in a relationship can be jeopardized, because both are being vulnerable, and vulnerability, like intimacy, is often very frightening to us. Many people have relationships which are basically shallow, rooted in things and in consuming, rather than in caring. To live life deeply, you *must* take the risks of getting hurt in order to have life's extreme joys. Life's joys are worth the risks of the pain that may come from living deeply.

Yet, looking at the same issues in a different way, the Chinese philosophers and sages say that the ideal to achieve in life is *balance.* Even in the moments of your greatest success, they counsel, don't become so ecstatic that you lose your center; and in the moments of greatest pain, don't become so despondent that you lose your good sense. These philosophers counsel us to keep an even view of things through success and failure— through the peaks and the valleys. If you have a deep perspective *within* yourself, they say, then even the simplest things can be very rich for you. For someone who has the sensitivity of a child, just walking through a field could be totally exciting. Whereas some adults become so numb that they need to shoot their bodies full of drugs or get drunk just to experience a little bit of "happiness."

The tenderness of the child allows it to be so open that the slightest thing—a whisper, a feather, a cat walking by—is a totally absorbing and exciting event. The child lives in a naked and totally new world. One of the qualities that characterizes the child's world is softness. A child's skin is so soft, his eyes are so huge. Everything about the child's body and being is soft and pliable. And it interacts with life that way. Things tickle, and the child giggles; when its feelings hurt, it cries. Most "adults" don't —because they no longer feel. And the child isn't programmed toward goals. It's willing to change its mind instantly, to go from crying to laughing in an instant. Young children are nearly always in the here and now. And so, in that sense, the child is having a constant relationship with its world, characterized by spontaneity, tenderness, and flow.

As children we were all exquisitely tender and sensitive. I can recall that when I was a child certain foods tasted very pungent on my tongue. For example, I could always detect hot foods—even the slightest bit of pepper. I'd say, "That has pepper on it, I don't want to eat it!" I was so sensitive to taste then, yet now my taste buds have become relatively insensitive after the period of time spent eating hot foods and Army "chow."

The usual numbing processes we generally accept without resistance. Most of us have numbed many parts of our bodies to protect ourselves from the pain that life often inflicts on us. I can recall very vividly that as a child, whenever I took my clothes off, my body was so sensitive to the air's caress that I would become sexually aroused. Just being naked was an erotic experience for me then. Now it takes another person, and sometimes she has to be naked, too. I may not be less sensitive sexually now, but I am less innocent.

School is a major numbing experience for the child whose creativity is sensitive and delicate.

Dr. Burton White of Harvard has been studying creativity in preschool children for the last decade. He has found that between the ages of eight and twenty-two months the child is literally consumed by curiosity. This is also the period when we tend to turn off the child's curiosity. At this age the child is reaching for all the breakable objects around and we say, "No, no, no!"—with a little slap on the hand to punctuate each no.

The child then gives up the reaching out, which is a very tender, honest, and innocent process for it. Dr. White has discovered that parents can be tender toward their children during this period and stimulate the child with "childproof" objects that won't be broken easily.

This allows the child's innate curiosity to blossom. Another inhibitor of a child's curiosity can be older brothers and sisters. The siblings who are a year or so older tend to overexaggerate the admonitions, the no's of the parents. This stamps out even more of the child's curiosity. Young children need some time and space away from their older brothers and sisters during this crucial period of development.

When I was working with gifted and talented children, parents would phone me and ask how to teach their two-year-old gifted children to read. My advice was, not to force them to read, but rather to allow that motivation to come from within them. We all have different cycles, inner clocks, and biorhythms. Some of us are morning people, others are evening people. If you force a morning person to perform in the evening, or vice versa, you will find that the performance will suffer significantly.

Parents need to allow their children the opportunity to learn to read more than words. There is also the wind, the scent of the forest and the sea to read, and the expressions on people's faces, their body language, and the total human environment. (And in our own relationships we need to allow that same space for our partners.) The motivation to read the words to express these feelings will flow quite naturally and more rapidly than our programmed, linear, lockstep systems will force it to. We need to surround children (and one another) with as much awareness as we can.

You can create a tender relationship with another person by seeing that the other person is really a lot like you, and that all the ways in which we are different can be invitations, not barriers. Our differences can be viewed as bonuses, new ways for us to discover one another. Your curiosity about these differences can become an endless source of fascination for both you and your partner. If there is something that your mate knows nothing about, the simple fact that you are interested in it can make it interesting to him or to her. They can watch you and learn. If you're involved with someone who likes to draw, for example, and you don't think you have any artistic talent, you may not want to explore drawing at first, but you can simply sit and watch your friend. The mere fact that you already love that person can transform his or her retreat into a private world of drawing into a fascinating experience for you as you watch. You become a silent witness to your partner, just by being there. It is important not to force yourself to do what your friend does. Nor do you need to compete with her or him. Simply let yourself *be* there with the person, and participate silently in what he or she does.

Enjoy your partner's pleasure. Such moments can create truly intimate times.

The Characteristics of the Tender Relationship

Earlier in this book, four traits were presented which Dr. Carl Rogers and his associates have found in their research to be present in any effective therapist. Some of Dr. Rogers' colleagues, including Dr. David Aspy, have since verified that the same four traits are also present in the effective teacher, or "learning facilitator." I'm convinced from my own experience in the federal government, the academic world, and in business that these traits are vital to effectiveness in most walks of life. I also feel that these four traits are the ones that lead to effective and tender relationships.

The four traits of good therapists which I have cited previously also have great value as vital aspects of any successful, tender relationship. The first trait is *genuineness*, on the part of both partners and toward the relationship itself. This means that neither of them is playing a role, but both are allowing themselves to be who they are, with their strengths and their weaknesses and all they bring to the relationship.

Sometimes one of their strengths will make up for a weakness of the other and create a sense of balance, a yin and yang, to the relationship. This genuineness is crucial to the effective and tender relationship. The partners must be willing to take off their masks and be there together as human beings sharing their aspirations, fears, joys, and sorrows.

There is a beautiful definition of realness in Margery Williams' beautiful book *The Velveteen Rabbit.* Nowadays there are many sensitive children's books which contain important messages for adults as well. This is one:

"What is REAL?" asked the Rabbit one day. "Does it mean having things that buzz inside of you, and a stick-out handle?" "REAL isn't how you were made," said the Skin Horse. "It's a thing that happens to you. When a child loves you for a long time, not just to play with, but really loves you, then you become REAL." "Does it hurt?" asked the Rabbit." "Sometimes," said the Skin Horse, for he was always truthful. "When you are REAL, you don't mind being hurt." "Does it happen all at once like being wound up," he asked, "or bit by bit?" "It doesn't happen all at once," said the Skin Horse. "You become. It takes a long time. That's why it doesn't often happen to people who break easily, or have sharp edges or who have to be carefully kept. Generally, by the time you are REAL, most of your hair has been loved off, and your eyes drop out and you get loose in the joints and very shabby. But these things don't matter at all, because once you are REAL, you can't be ugly, except to people who don't understand. . . . Once you are REAL, you can't become unreal again. It lasts for always."*

*Margery Williams, *The Velveteen Rabbit* (New York: Doubleday & Company, Inc.), pp. 16–20.

So the first trait which is essential to the tender relationship is a sense of realness between the partners.

The second trait they must share is a sense of *prizing* each other—really caring about each other, enough to celebrate the uniqueness of each other as separate, precious human beings. This is the opposite of apathetic sophistication. It is what caring is all about, and what any lasting relationship requires.

The third trait of the tender relationship is *empathetic understanding*—being able to put yourself in the other person's experience, to see from the other's viewpoint. To be able to see things the way the other person sees them is often difficult for us. When we are arguing with our partners, it can be useful to try to restate their points of view as though they were coming from them. Doing this almost inevitably increases the "tenderness quotient" in the communication we are sharing.

The process of doing this helps in itself. It helps to create empathy, which is one of the traits found to be essential to the effective therapist, to the effective teacher, and which I feel is also one of the characteristics of a tender relationship.

A fourth trait of the tender relationship is a *sense of trust.* Trust can grow largely from these other three traits, but it is something that often takes a while to nurture.

There may be more trust during the initial period of the relationship than later. We need to return to that innocent stage when we really trusted the other person. This is difficult after scars have formed from the hurts which develop in every relationship.

Trust comes from knowing that the other person is there not to compete against you or to do you in, but rather is allied with you against the other forces which may infringe upon your relationship. So it's standing *together* side by side looking outward together, instead of face to face *against* each other.

In addition to these four traits identified by Carl Rogers and his associates, there are other traits which I feel characterize the tender relationship. A *sense of humor* is one. Laughing with each other, particularly in the most strained or tenuous times, can break the tension and enable the tenderness within each of us to facilitate communication. After our armor has been set aside, we can laugh together instead of *at* each other. Learning to laugh at ourselves is one way to defuse the tension in a relationship. It can lead to more tenderness.

Have you ever seen a little puppy that barks and scares itself? The puppy barks and jumps back two feet, not knowing he could make such a noise. He scares himself with all his seriousness. I find that I need to laugh at myself at times when I take myself too seriously. A sense of humor provides ballast to any good and long-term relationship.

Another aspect of the tender relationship is some sense of *tradition and ritual.* There are certain preferred ways that we all do things. Athletes, for example, when things are going well for them, will wear the same socks every day, or use the same baseball bat, or put the left shoe on first all the time, or follow some other little ritual that makes them feel that they are putting their energy through the same kinds of channels. For example, if you go into a particular room to meditate, and use that space just for that purpose, after a while you'll notice that whenever you go into the room the energy you have put into the room is still there. And that feeds you and strengthens your meditation or whatever it is that you are doing in the room. Or you can go into someone's house and immediately, even before you meet them, you can feel their energy in the room. If you are aware of your environment, you can absorb it, not only by observing how the room is decorated, but simply by feeling what the emotional tone of the room is.

Often, you can feel more in a very old room, in an old house where there has been so much more experience of living than in a new home or building. When I go into new houses now, I feel very uncomfortable. There's something in the building materials, in the very newness of them, that bothers me. There's no feeling that any other people have lived there before. There's no aliveness, no feeling or tone.

One way to create a special environment is to establish rituals in your relationships. Perhaps it is saying grace before a meal, a simple ritual that quiets everything down, just as snow quiets when it falls, making everything softer and more silent. In the same way, no matter how hungry you are before you sit down to a meal, if you just stop for a moment and know that everyone around the table is doing the same thing, then you can all share a precious moment together. You know that everyone is sharing the same silence. This kind of ritual creates a space for people to feel that their softer emotions have a place in the relationship. This is not necessarily a religious practice, but it does create a space for the spirit element in our lives to be present with us in a continuing way.

A *sense of history* is also vital. People can develop a history in ten minutes together. Their history then has nine-plus minutes of history and one moment of the present. In ten days together, ten months together, or ten years, your history obviously gets longer and richer. Your history is like a sea anchor in the stormy seas of life. Life will toss and turn you. A sea anchor gives your boat stability, yet doesn't impede its progress. The longer your history is, the stronger your sea anchor. It holds you steady in the face of life's storms and high winds.

History isn't all pleasant, and there will be scars from some of the unpleasant times, just as there are many joys in your mutual history. Tradition is a way of keeping your history alive as you go back and remember those moments and give them renewed life. In time, they become rituals. It's a good feeling to feel the security of our history again, celebrating annual holidays together, perhaps decorating the tree a special way, or having certain rituals during vacation times. For me, experiencing wild geese each year when they fly south for the winter has become a very important part of my history. Returning to the same lake in New Hampshire where I spent all my childhood summers and where roots exist for me has been a powerful sea anchor in an otherwise turbulent life. Sharing these traditions with a partner can be a very tender and special experience. Your history then becomes shared, and as you develop a common history, it can help you to reach the tenderness in your relationship which provides you both stability and sensitivity.

When I am with a friend, that friend and I share our own history. The richness of joint memories creates for us a specialness and tenderness in our relationship. All of us have a history together from events we have shared in the past. We create it continuously. And every act we live is a very precious act. To spend a day of your life with a person is perhaps the most precious gift you can give him. There will never be another one exactly like it. It's unique—if you experience it this way. If not, it's just a day, just an afternoon, just another empty expanse of time "to kill."

To spend a lifetime with another human being is an incredible thing to contemplate. Intermingling your energies and your experiences over an entire life span gives both of you— whether friends or mates—a living history that pervades your time together with the scents and essences of your past, increasing the richness of the present for both of you.

To feel secure and safe enough with another person, to want to be totally open and honest together, is a rare and wonderful expression of your love. Yet there are rare occasions when openness, ideal as it seems, can be used as a weapon.

At times, we think we are opening and sharing with our partners, when we are really "dumping," not sharing. There are events in our lives which are really private. To unload these on someone else merely relieves us of some of the burden while imposing it on them. So, total openness, though desirable most of the time, on occasions is counterproductive. For example, occasional images in our minds or fantasies are sometimes best kept to ourselves. It is fulfilling to feel free enough to share uninhibitedly with another person, but at certain times, if done promiscuously, to share our experience so uncritically can be painful.

When we have a nagging or persistent thought, idea, or piece of information which we fear to open to our partner, it can impede and cloud much of our communication. This does not occur so much intellectually—as words are a form of precise, controlled communication—as it does emotionally and spiritually. The small fleeting or insignificant thoughts or one-time-only events that will disappear rather than persist if not opened are at times better kept to ourselves rather than unloaded on our partners.

If we take the risk of opening to our partners those persistent things that keep coming back to us, then often that can remove the cloudiness and bring us much closer to the other person. However, if we are opening threatening things, we have to be ready to bear the brunt of our partners' emotional reactions—perhaps their anger—if they are hurt. To open up *everything* to *everyone* else indiscriminately is not only undesirable, but can be a cruel and hateful thing to do. We can humiliate someone with honesty just as we can honor them with honesty. There is a great difference between dumping and sharing.

Another characteristic of the tender relationship is that *it nourishes both people.* It does not exhaust them. Though the relationship has peaks and valleys, it also has a steady river of strength that runs through it all the time, to which both partners can return and from which they can draw a real and continuing nourishment. From that place they can then go out and venture into the forest to explore exciting new trails together. But they can always hear the river flowing, and they know they are never very far from it.

A useful exercise for partners is just to be with each other in a room. Men and women particularly often feel that when they are together they have to be "doing" something. The man has to be showing the woman how much he cares for her, or the woman has to be showing the man how special he is. This becomes a constant and tiring battle for attention, or a constant need for one to prove him- or herself to the other, instead of being willing just to be there, trusting that the way you are is O.K., and letting the other person know that he or she is also O.K. The exercise you can do to begin to break through some of the barriers that we all have (like our sense of embarrassment that being with someone and not saying anything is wrong) is just to sit in front of your partner and look into his or her left eye for a while. As you do this, you may begin to notice some things begin to happen. For example, you may see beyond the surface of your partner's face to the inner being. The face before you may suddenly become very soft and glowing. You may even see light around the face. You won't have to look for it; you will be just looking into the eye of your partner, and you may notice this light that's coming off your partner's face. And, although you can't see it, it's also emanating from *you.*

The face you are watching may begin to change. At times, I have had the experience of looking at my partner and then feeling that I am able to see inside of her face. Perhaps my partner has a very pained expression or an angry expression and I am able by looking into her eyes to see something suddenly shift and her face soften as I see softly what is inside her pain. At times, I may see something that she already feels she is expressing—sadness or hurt or well-being.

But what always comes through is this incredible human beauty that's always waiting inside each of us if we are only patient and tender enough to get to that place with each other by doing this simplest of things—just looking into each other's eyes.

We send each other an incredible amount of energy through our eyes. Light is the strongest source of energy, yet so soft, so subtle, almost invisible. Without it, we wouldn't be able to see anything, or even to exist. Everything we eat is transformed sunlight. If you try this exercise, allow yourself to just be there with the other person. Let your awareness begin to melt and join the other person's in a wordless moment. Often it can be deeper and simpler than many sexual experiences. Doing this exercise, you can feel the incredible power that we all have, which somehow isn't expressed in our words or even necessarily in our actions. We have the power. What we don't always have is the *awareness* of just how deep and thrilling this power can be. Doing this exercise can help you to raise your tenderness quotient—your awareness of your own power and beauty.

We are not always able to summon up all that energy and put it into a single act or a single statement. Yet it's always there waiting to be tapped if we can slow ourselves down and be patient enough with ourselves. You might try the same exercise with yourself sometime—by looking into a mirror. For many, many years when I was a child, I used to look into a mirror and get lost in my own eyes. It gave me an incredible feeling of strength, a feeling that, no matter what anybody thought, I knew my own inner depths.

Another important characteristic of the tender relationship is *being willing to accept the other person exactly as he or she is,* rather than feeling that you are going to change him or her. It doesn't really work to try to change other people. You are taking liberties with them that you have no right to take. What does work is to accept them, and to give them the space to be the way they really are. What you may find then is that they will begin to change just from feeling free enough to be themselves. When they no longer have to defend who they are against your expectations, the natural process of growth that is deep inside all of us will take over.

If we can learn to be more patient and more tender with each other, we may discover the true depths inside us *all*—and then realize that we already *are* exactly the way we've always wanted ourselves and each other to be. So this aspect of a tender relationship is being willing to accept your partner for who he or she is. And being willing to accept yourself for who you are.

When you are willing to accept other people, then you will also find that you will be unwilling to allow other people to judge you or to try to change you. You will be creating more freedom for yourself, just as you are helping others create more freedom for themselves. If you do this, you'll have more space to enjoy your relationships with other people, and your relationships with them will be characterized less by a sense of forcing and more by a sense of tenderness and flow.

Another characteristic of the tender relationship is *vulnerability,* and this is so important that it is discussed in considerably more detail in the next chapter. When two people in a relationship are willing to take the risks of disarming, seeing past their shells and their masks, and becoming vulnerable with each other, true intimacy can result. It is one of the major defining characteristics of the tender relationship. It is our fear of being emotionally naked and spontaneous which keeps us outside the door to intimacy. Our willingness to be vulnerable is one of the keys by which we can enter the endless space which we call "love."

9 Vulnerability: The Gateway to Intimacy

Intimacy is a state of union in which the boundaries that usually divide people seem to disappear. According to Webster, "intimate" means "Intrinsic, essential . . . belonging to or characterizing one's deepest nature." When we are intimate with someone, we share this "deepest nature." Yet intimacy is something many of us fear—particularly macho males.

Why is it that we fear this so much? What could be as fulfilling?

When we are intimate, we open ourselves to the great pain and hurt that might result if our relationship with another does not fare well. To protect ourselves from that anxiety we arm ourselves, like belligerent nations or feuding families. We keep our distance, even in the relationship. We relate on intellectual or physical levels, at arm's length, but we avoid the emotional or spiritual communications which might lead us to intimacy under less defended postures. Of course, by doing this we also protect ourselves from the greatest possible joy and tenderness —that of being intimate with another human being.

The experience or process of intimacy is something I have had much trouble with in my own life. I get along well with a wide variety of people: on a safe level, an intellectual level. I am quite skilled at playing society's defined roles in the various dramas of life. But in the relationships which really matter—those that offer the promise of emotional and spiritual fulfill-ment—I have not always fared so well. I attribute that failure in intimate relationships to my failure to be in touch with my tenderness. By protecting myself from pain with toughness, I create a barrier between myself and others, across which physical and intellectual communication can flow with little diffi-culty, but over which little if any emotional or spiritual flow can pass. Accordingly, there has been very little intimacy in my life, while at the same time I have hungered deeply for it. The protective moat I built around myself was more subconscious than conscious. For many of us, I think, the nightmare of child-hood causes us to build up our subconscious defenses against more pain or more rejection.

Now I am discovering that the key to intimacy for me is vulnerability. When I am vulnerable, I am more apt to let down my defenses and experience the quivering, delicate joy of inti-mately relating with another in a tender and unprotected way. It is true that I open myself to the possible hurt and pain of rejection. But the joys of intimacy are worth the risk that I may be hurt. Better to feel pain than to feel nothing at all.

The part of me that is really "in love" is the part of me that is tender, that cries, that is imperfect, unprotected, and vulner-able. It is also the part of me that others love—when I make it available. Love always wants to share itself. By being spontane-ous and vulnerable, we set it free so that it can join us to others.

Concessions and Obligations

There is a destructive game we play in relationships that keeps us apart. I call this game "Concessions." Instead of work-ing things out to a mutually agreeable solution or planning an event together, we make concessions to one another, thereby creating a "one-up" in our favor on the obligation ledger. I can remember making many such concessions to my first wife. For example, once she wanted us to buy a house I didn't particularly care for. Since she really wanted the security of our own house, I conceded to her and we bought it. Having conceded to her, I felt she owed me something considerable!

Frequently when you ask a friend if he'd like to do something with you, like go fishing, you'll get the response "I'd love to, but you know how it is; the wife hasn't seen me much lately, and I owe it to her and the children to spend Sunday with them." What a condescending statement! He's making a "concession" to spend time with his family!

It's refreshing to get the strong, honest response from someone centered enough to say, "No, thanks, I want to be with my family Sunday." That's taking responsibility for oneself instead of using as an excuse the "superior"-sounding denigration of the family. (The implication is "It's their fault that I can't go fishing with you. Blame them, not me.") Such a concession is irresponsible. Rather than the concession, I'd prefer to hear the honest response "Good idea! I need to get away from the family for a break. I'll go." As I write this, I'm aware that when I blame my family, as I have done in similar situations, I don't feel strong or good. When I take responsibility for my actions or statements, I feel strong, I like myself, and I feel good.

There's a fine but definite line between concessions and compromises. Compromises don't have the strings or obligations tied to them that concessions have. Also, compromises are made between equal parties. When I concede, it has a superiority tinge to it that degrades the person I am conceding to. A compromise is more of a contract in which both parties give up something in order to gain something. There is a parity of balance. Concessions leave one party unbalanced, owing the other something.

Repeated conceding in a marriage or love relationship can be an insidious process. Always conceding about what I'll have for dinner, where I'll go for vacations, what car I'll buy, or whom I'll invite to visit is giving up my rights and denying my own importance as an individual in such a way as to get the other party to owe me a great debt of gratitude or love or whatever it is I need and am after. Huge resentments lurk at the end of the concession game. Yet I can't make someone pay off these "debts," just as I can't make anyone love me. I may suppose that they are deeply in debt to me for all that I have conceded to them, but actually these concessions just get in the way of their being free with me.

Our Western world is hung up on obligations. We are always "owing" people and incurring obligations. If I invite someone over for dinner, they feel obligated to invite me to their house, not necessarily because they enjoy being with me, but because they "owe me." Even love becomes something we withhold, barter, invest, or owe. Eastern society, and in particular the Hindu culture, has a tradition called the "Non-giving of Gifts," in which no psychological obligations are created in giving a gift. Nothing is owed. Only the spirit of giving is shared.

When I give something to someone, I want it to be because I want to give it. The sense of "no obligation" can be illustrated by passing the pen I am writing with from my right hand to my left hand. My left hand doesn't owe my right hand anything in exchange for receiving the pen, because both hands belong to the same body, hence no obligations. There can be a similar sense of unity in a relationship with another person. Both persons belong to a larger "body"—the relationship they share and through which they share themselves with each other.

I believe that the more intimate the relationship we have with parents when we are children—especially in the earliest years, months, even hours—the more apt we are to experience intimacy as adults, without fearing the pain of rejection or requiring emotional I.O.U.'s. To be taken away from the softness and nurture of a mother's breast is the harshest of rejections. It is too painful for us to experience as infants, so we begin to collect calluses over our delicate feelings to avoid that primal pain. It happens to us all, though some are more fortunate to have been held at the breast longer than others. Even if not breast fed, most of us were at least held, fondled, and stroked by loving mothers and fathers during a significant number of hours in infanthood and childhood. Soon, however, we are taught that the material rewards of society will come to us abundantly only if we continue to toughen ourselves competitively, in school and later in our careers. And the punishments come even more readily than the rewards if we do not compete or if we march to our own drumbeat. Small wonder, then, that our tenderness is forced beneath our invisible shells!

Surrendering As a Medicine for Lovers' Fights

The capability of surrendering seems to be crucial to accepting. I am discovering that conditioning as a macho male is virtually incompatible with the concept of surrender. When I can surrender to a loved one, to a friend, to a student, I can accept them and not have to debate or engage in combat. They do not have to become "the enemy."

During a particularly trying time in my relationship with my wife, we discovered two things that have helped us to avoid escalating arguments into all-out disasters. The first one is not to treat each other like the enemy. If we can stop for a moment and each let the other know that he or she is not the target, not the enemy in what is going on, we can care more about each other and sometimes even work out our differences.

The second thing that has helped us is being open and vulnerable with each other about our feelings. This means admitting to each other that we feel anxious, scared, fearful, sad, lonely, or that we were wrong about something on which we took a righteous stand. This, of course, is virtually impossible if one of us is treating the other like the enemy.

These two guidelines, though they may seem elementary, have become important to us in working out what often seem to be impossible communication difficulties. The defensive shell that is put up against someone who is treating you like the enemy is virtually impossible to penetrate. The two guidelines work in tandem. You can't treat someone like the enemy on the one hand and still be open and vulnerable about your feelings on the other. Being open and vulnerable isn't possible when waging war.

A corollary to these two guidelines for de-escalating an argument is the same as that for de-escalating a war: disarmament. If one party will take the risk of making what I call a "self-disarming statement," it goes a long way toward defusing an argument. When I arm myself for battle with someone, I often escalate the argument by counterattacking against whatever attack I feel has been made on me. Example: SHE: "Don't shout at me like that, you male chauvinist." Now, I could escalate this one fact with a dozen appropriate rejoinders. However to *de*-escalate the argument is the trickier job. An honest self-disarming statement often does the trick. Example: HE: "I'm sorry I was shouting; I am feeling anxious about something I'd like to share with you."

Sometimes it appears a big risk to disarm when the other seems to be on the offensive, but the vulnerability of an honest self-disarming statement is usually a far better response than either a defensive or a counterattacking offensive reply. Try it out. I hope you'll find it works for you, as it often does for me, when little else seems to be helping.

All of this is akin to surrendering to the other person or, more important, surrendering to your feelings. While I used to be inclined to wear a red, white, and blue American flag on my lapel, I am beginning to wear a white flag to remind me to surrender more often.

My capacity to surrender is tied directly to my inner tenderness or vulnerable feelings, while my striving to be the perfect person really reflects my tough armor or surface shell: an invincible image.

When two loved ones are hassling and squabbling and no efforts to communicate seem to help, disarmament down to a completely unprotected state can be the act that opens the sluice gates of love and intimacy. Certainly this is a real risk for one to take, but vulnerability works with a loved one as a key to intimacy even when the battle is going full force. When my wife and I are near the violent stage of a fight, I find that, rather than taking on a counteroffensive or an impregnable defensive role, if I look beyond her hostility and defensive armament to her hurt and fear, to the tender part within—or if I smile or cry or do whatever flows naturally—then often we can melt intimately together and put our spears and shields aside.

Vulnerability: High Risk with Lovers, Low Risk with Strangers

When I surrender to my feelings for another person rather than try to "program" my behavior, I find that I am more able to let down my protective guard and flow naturally. This natural flow is relatively unprotected and uncensored. It is the "real" me rather than a person playing a role. This real me is capable of intimacy with other special people. I say "special" people because intimacy is not something I particularly desire with everyone. I reserve this risk of being vulnerable, which carries with it the risk of being hurt, for those special persons about whom I care a great deal. Yet being vulnerable is even more risky with the special persons, inasmuch as rejection from them would be so very painful.

In recent years I have often found myself spontaneously opening myself before large groups of people, in speeches, or on TV, and in my writings for publication. I know I enjoy the closeness I often feel with many members of the audience on such occasions or with those who write warm letters in response to my writings or speeches. That is specifically the reason why I agree to speak as often as I do. I certainly wouldn't care enough about it to give speeches if I didn't get something in return from the people I address. And though there are usually several people in a large audience with whom I feel a special empathy and from whom I derive a great deal of energy, there are also others whom I observe being uncomfortable when I open myself vulnerably in a speech. I can sense their discomfort as they look away from me or close themselves off from me and the pain my personal experience may trigger in them. The thing I share with them in those moments, even though they may tune me out with their pain, is our deep mutual loneliness —and within that loneliness is the potential for intimacy. If we become vulnerable within ourselves, which we do when we allow ourselves to experience our own loneliness, we also experience a great intimacy with ourselves. We become whole again.

I was asked recently how I could take such a risk opening myself vulnerably before large groups of strangers. As I searched for the answer, I realized that vulnerability with strangers doesn't have nearly the risk that vulnerability has with a loved one. If strangers dislike you in any way, it is not so painful. If a loved one rejects you, the pain is almost unbearable. For the macho male this leads to repeated shallow relationships with

different women. He takes few risks in having a sexual relationship—potentially the most intimate of relationships—with
someone who is nearly a stranger. If a stranger rejects him, it
is not so painful. But it is just as lonely.

Multiple Relationships As a Defense Against Intimacy

Having many sexual relationships is often a defense against
having real intimacy with one person. If one or two or more of
the shallow relationships go sour, we still have others to fall back
on. It is a great risk to put everything into only one intimate
relationship with another special human being, without reserve
relationships to fall back on if that one should fail. Yet this high
risk also has its own special rewards. It gives our lives a stability
which frees us to explore higher levels of achievement, awareness, and sharing.

At times in my life I have found that I can be "in love" with
more than one person at the same time. I have also met other
men (and women) who find this to be true in their lives. I have
also found this to be a very difficult road to travel, however. One
crucial thing about my capacity to love more than one person
is simply the amount of energy I have available. The more love
relationships I tried to sustain, the more I diluted my energy
and my capacity to give to any one person. For example, when
I was single I found myself attempting to sustain three or four
love relationships of varying intensities. What I discovered was
that I was not really able to give—or to receive—enough emotional or physical nourishment in any one of these relationships.
Moreover, even without the press of time, I suspect that I do not
have the emotional or physical energy to give as much as I
would like to more than one. It's easy to have sex with many
more people than one can adequately love. But it dilutes one's
energy and capacity to give to those he or she loves.

There will be those who disagree with me, and yet I have never seen in any marriage relationship one or both partners enter into multi-love relationships successfully and still preserve a truly genuine, deep relationship with each other without great pain and suffering on the part of both partners. This has been my own personal experience as well.

Most of my life I have been very shy and inhibited about saying to anyone, "I love you." I recall how I refrained from making this verbal commitment even in my West Point days, when most of my classmates were telling their dates the magic words "I love you" because women just wouldn't "go far" in those days without that. Though I have made love with many women, I can count on one hand the number of women I have told I loved. Somehow this was a sacred "once in a lifetime" experience I was waiting for. I was never sure that the good, pleasurable feelings were really love. Perhaps my spiritual and emotional development was so delayed that I was incapable of love in those days. On the other hand, my perception that I really wasn't in love may have been accurate at that time. Now that I am growing to be more of a whole man, with spiritual, emotional, intellectual, and physical cylinders all occasionally hitting at the same time, love is possible for me to experience. I am not so conservative about expressing or experiencing the full beauty and joy (and yes, the pain) of love.

Another thing I'm discovering is that I don't just love someone with "blanket" love. I dislike and even hate some things about some of the people I love. This doesn't cause me to feel that I have to reject them. It frees me from being forced to say to a loved one, as so many feel compelled to do, "I love you, but I hate this thing you've done, so get out of my life!" The fact is that I like some things and dislike others about everyone I know or love, including myself.

Though I've been accused of being a romantic, I don't really believe that "love blinds." For me, and for many people, the traditional concepts of love cause us to refuse to accept consciously the things we dislike or hate about our loved ones. Hence, we sublimate our dislikes, pushing them out of our consciousness. But they are very much down there, manifesting themselves in other ways—disguised as resentments, aggressions, or other hostile behavior.

Our energies can be concentrated in much the same way as a magnifying glass will concentrate the sun's rays to ignite a paper. The greatest athletes experience this when they summon their adrenaline and energy to explode through the line in a football game or gather themselves to put the shot. I can remember watching a fellow cadet on the track team, Bob Kyasky, an amazing athlete who knew how to concentrate his energy like no one I have ever seen. Though he was a great football player, he was plagued with an ankle injury, which was perhaps the only thing that kept him from being one of football's all-time greats. Still he could explode "off tackle" with phenomenal energy and speed. On the track team he would easily win the 100- and 220-yard dashes, and then he would rest up a few minutes until time to make the last call for the high jump, bypassing all of the earlier elimination jumps. I used to watch him with awe as, while lacing on his jumping shoes, he would gather and focus all the life forces within him, getting ready to concentrate them in one leap over the six-foot bar. The seconds before the leap were filled with intense concentration. Then, with hands shaking free, eyes on the bar, and energy all flowing to the "springs" in his legs, he would take three quick light steps and explode up and over the bar!

If you find yourself spreading yourself too thin in a defense against real intimacy with one person, ask yourself which relationship is most special to you. Perhaps several people will be special in different ways. If one emerges, try to open yourself as much as you can with that one person. Let down your protective guard. Peck out of your shell. Be your real self. Flow into the frightening but freeing abyss of intimacy.

You may find that the other person is also afraid of intimacy. Share your fear. Tell the other person of the risk you feel you are taking. (At times when I do this I discover I am really warning them, "Please be careful with me. I am going to be vulnerable with you.") Also share with them the fact that you want intimacy with them and that being vulnerable can be your shared key to greater intimacy.

Doing this will also cause you to learn what it is you value in your relationships. Having to narrow down the recipients of your energy will cause you to make some hard choices about whom you're going to spend your time and energy with. This can help you to see through some of the confusion that usually accompanies the piecemealing of energy that we often engage in.

By taking the risk, you may find (as I did when I tried this) a new richness and ecstasy that you and your partner had deprived yourselves of in the past by diluting your energies. Vulnerability and tenderness can lead to intimacy. And intimacy leads to love. Like sunlight concentrated by the glass, concentrated love does more than cause a fitful or brief stirring of the heart. Love in its concentrated power will bring on that supreme fever which can enkindle your entire being.

On Blending, Centering, and Flowing with Others

Tenderness springs from flowing. It is impeded and thwarted by thrashing and struggling. George Leonard, the author, once shared with me some of the lessons he was then learning in the Oriental martial art of aikido. Aikido is a Japanese art of self-defense which employs the principle of nonresistance and uses an opponent's own momentum against him. But it is much more than that. It is also a discipline of utilizing the mind, body, and spirit to channel one's own energy flow.

A master is set upon by four attackers simultaneously, and the secret of his survival is his ability to flow with each—a delicate and complex art, to say the least. Instead of taking each head-on, he flows and blends with their motions. He becomes one with them, like an extension of them.

I attended a workshop which George Leonard led for a group of government officials in Washington, D.C., during which we participated in an exercise which helped us "see" the practical applications of flowing. We were asked to stand at one end of a room while our partners stood and presented obstacles in the middle of the room. Our objective was to walk a straight line through the obstacles (a hand, foot, or body) presented at the last second as we passed our partners on our way to a chair at the other end of the room. One attempt was to be made after concentration on getting there "no matter what"—the typical "I'll do it, come hell or high water" persistence of the "success-ful," tough American male. In this exercise we found that we would usually crash into the obstacles our partners presented and after a violent struggle, we would finally succeed in reach-ing the goal. During another attempt we were to concentrate on a passive "I wish I hadn't gotten out of bed" attitude and proceed to the objective. We invariably found our way blocked and few succeeded in reaching the goal. A third attempt was made. This time we concentrated on "centering" ourselves in our energy centers—a few inches below our navels, from where our strength flows. Now we were peaceful, gentle, tender human beings flowing toward our objective. In this situation, no matter how hard our partners tried to obstruct us (they didn't know which of the three states—determined, passive or flowing —we'd be using each time), we found we would flow or even dance gracefully through them to our objective with little struggle or violence. The implications for all of us in our work, with our supervisors, or in our relationships with others were dynamically apparent.

Soft Eyes

George Leonard also shared with me the concept of "soft eyes." The overachieving macho male often glares at things with great intensity as if to overcome them or outdo or conquer them. "Seeing with soft eyes" is a tender way of seeing that can help us to flow. It is an allowing "seeing" rather than a penetrating "looking."

What is the difference between "seeing" and "looking"? Looking has an evaluative aspect to it. The overachiever is continually "looking" hard at things, trying hard to figure or sort them out. It is a "head tripping" intellectual process of evaluating or classifying people instead of just letting them be there.

Often the overachiever actually becomes myopic and needs glasses from continually straining his eye muscles in his efforts to look into things better. My own nearsightedness is probably a result of my West Point training for trying harder and overachieving. Some actually have done away with glasses after learning in therapy to "see" rather than to "look." Contrasted with this "looking" is "seeing"—a here-and-now process much like "grokking," the term used in the science fiction novel *Stranger in a Strange Land,* by Robert Heinlein. Grokking and seeing appear to avoid the intellectual classifying, and connect "mainline" from eyes to heart rather than from eyes to brain. It is a sensing, not an intellectualizing. And it means accepting the person you "see," rather than judging the person you "look" at.

George Leonard's idea of "soft eyes" is very similar. We tenderly soften our gaze from the hard stare we so often use to protect ourselves. It is a vulnerable step at first, but then it can lead to a centered flowing with others in such a way that even if they are hostile, it can help to disarm them.

"Seeing" our partners rather than "looking" at them can help to "tenderize" our relationship, dissolve our mutual toughness, and broaden our mutual trust. I found recently that when I am fly fishing on a trout stream, if I use "soft eyes" I can see in the water literally hundreds of well camouflaged trout which elude me if I fight hard to look at them. This helps me when a trout rises to my fly. I flow with the trout and the stream and become one with them. I also find that "soft eyes" enable me to see deer in the forest which often evade my "looking" stare. It's a flowing with or becoming a part of nature in a tender way rather than opposing or going against her in an invading way. The softer I become, the more I can see in nature, and the more she has to show me.

The Maze of Love

Love is such a paradox. It is easy to intellectualize and talk about, yet experiencing and understanding it often defies us. It is unendingly complex, yet so incredibly simple if we would only flow with it.

An image which helps me to understand my loving relationship with my partner is to see it in the form of mazes. Imagine that you are a maze with complex compartments eventually leading to your center. Your partner is a different maze. If you take the wrong doors, you end up at dead ends instead of at your center. When a love relationship begins between you and your partner, imagine that an area of your separate mazes is overlapping so that your centers coincide in the same place. As you enter each compartment of your maze, on the way to your "center," you must open each door with a separate key that only you possess. Since you have learned how to use your keys, you know how to negotiate the difficult maze to get to your center. But now that you have entered a love relationship, you find that your mazes overlap in one area but not everywhere. Part of your life and maze is separate from your partner's, and each of you alone may open the doors to your separate compartments with your own keys. When you get to the overlapping portions of your mazes, you find that you now can travel hand in hand with your lover—but wait. Your key alone is not able to open these shared doors. Your partner's key is also needed. So it takes two keys, yours and hers, to move together toward your common love center.

No matter how hard you want to progress, both keys are needed. If your partner is afraid to progress through the next door or doesn't want to go deeper, there is little you can do about it. You can't force the doors. You must use both keys. After you successfully learn the maze together, going deeper and deeper toward your common center, the place where you unite in love as one supreme being, you will always long to return there with your partner. It is such a beautiful place of shared boundless love and bliss. Yet as your relationship progresses, one of you may venture out of your center, perhaps too fast for your partner. Doors will be slammed. Disharmony and disagreement will result, which will occasionally lead to pain and hurt. These wounds can heal, but on later trips together into the maze you and your partner will recall the pain experienced in the past at one door or another when it was slammed shut and locked by one of you. This will cause some fear to arise within you as you approach each successive door.

It will take renewed courage to go deeper, knowing how it hurt the last time. Yet venture deeper. Few of us are willing to forfeit the bliss of our common centers, and explore only our own mazes alone.

This image of the maze helps me understand how I must progress step by step, key by key, jointly with my partner. At times we sail right through, our keys joyfully opening each door. At other times we are reluctant; one wants to go faster than the other, while one is fearful. One thinks he or she has lost or forgotten the correct key. But this never really happens. Once we have learned the maze, we know it. Fear of sharing such incredible intimacy and union is the only thing that blocks us. Our locksmith for the maze of love is really our tender inner self. This inner self knows exactly which key to use. When we are in touch with our inner selves, we can flow through the maze of love with no difficulty. The tender relationship is one in which both partners are relating center to center rather than wall to wall or maze to maze.

10 Tenderness in Sexuality

Reaching Your Inner Rhythms

In these times of widespread numbness, the erotic experience is one of the most direct and effective routes to our natural inner rhythms. In sexual experience—especially at the moment of orgasm—we experience a vulnerability and a tenderness that we allow ourselves at few other times. At these precious moments, we tap our mother lode of internal energy as it surfaces after being hidden safely beneath our veneers of toughness. This is true for most of us, including the macho male. Yet the quality of sexual experience for those who are in touch with their tenderness is much different than it is for those who wear toughness at all times, including in bed.

Sex is one of those subjects most men love to talk about—but not too much. Too much talk about sex makes men a little nervous; they get afraid they may find out they don't know as much as they suppose they do. And sex is something no man likes to feel stupid about.

So instead, often this macho talk becomes loud and vulgar,

with clever jokes about new positions and new prospects. In some ways, talking about sex becomes preferable to the act itself. It is easier, it often lasts longer, and there is rarely any disappointment. Men who are afraid to be aggressive in bed can invent marvelous nights along the bar with their comrades before they all go home to their grumpy wives who never see any of this incredible action.

It is so sad, and so unnecessary. These men often feel sick at heart because they are afraid they have failed as lovers. They walk around with a fantasy of "how it ought to be": all screams and whispers and fingernails and lips, sighs of "Darling, hold me" and "Oh, you're so fantastic," and then the white fire and the soft clouds carrying them out over a gentle far-off sea. . . . But they know it isn't anything like that when *they* get into bed; it is often confusing and lonely and painful. They feel trapped by their own ignorance, by their terrible fear of admitting just how little they really know, and by a society filled with glossy images and unreal expectations of sexual perfection, images which many of these men have internalized and from which they now cannot escape. They do not "make love" at all. They masturbate with these impossible fantasies, and then they blame themselves (or their sex partners) for their failure to achieve these unreal standards of air-brushed eroticism.

It is no wonder that the number of impotent males is rising so dramatically. Many men are no longer confident of their own sexuality. The overemphasis on the female orgasm—and on orgasm itself—has contributed to many men's fear of approaching women. There is a sense of judgment of performance which precedes sexual encounters now that is new and disturbing to many men. Women have fought for their sexual rights, and in many respects they have gained the upper hand in terms of their willingness to define what they want and what they will or will not do sexually. But men feel trapped by their traditional stance of being "in control." Machos don't have any sexual problems—everyone knows that. So men feel unable to admit their confusions, and they wind up being torn apart by the growing tension to perform sexually while being unsure as to their own real sexual wants.

Although this present phase of male-female relations is difficult and painful, for men no less than for women, it is serving a valuable function by breaking down many of the stereotypes which have protected (but not nourished) men in the past. The male ego is a brittle and fragile thing, as many men are beginning to realize. It demands constant propping up, constant attention; and it is constantly *in* tension. For the macho, sex is not an enjoyment as much as yet another test of his manhood. Every time, it is all on the line. All too frequently, it is not pleasure he seeks in his sex. It is performance.

Up to a point, this attitude actually makes him somewhat attractive as a lover. The women he attracts know that he will always try to put up a good show. And some women like that. Not necessarily because they like *him,* but because his good show validates *their* image and *their* show. He is the superstud, and they are the supersirens. The relationship works. The only trouble with it is that it doesn't go anywhere. It soon begins to require more and more energy just to maintain the same level of ego gratification: more times per night, wilder variations, madder music, and stronger wine or drugs. Very soon both parties may begin to realize that they are headed down a dead-end path. Yet the rules of their game prevent them from turning around. Very few machos give up their act. Very few sirens dress in calico. Instead, they find new partners to play out their games with. For the game must go on. There are no quitters in the Machismo Olympics—especially not in the sexual relays.

The result of this narrow approach to sexuality is a kind of hardness, in both men and women. In women it can be seen in their stiff lacquered hair, painted faces, and the carefully calibrated bras they wear to put up "a good front." And in men it is there in the rough language and fumbling gestures and hard eyes which assure them that they are coming on strong. (If they only knew.) This harness is the hardness of the ego, stiff and shell-like, which these men and women present to the world and to each other as their sorry substitute for aliveness and real interest. They aren't interested in each other. They are interested in peddling their ego shells for whatever they can get for them. They are like dolls trying to make contact yet getting no deeper than the painted porcelain exteriors they have so carefully arranged.

So, inevitably their sex is tough, just as they themselves are tough. The women demand more and more orgasms as a way of proving to themselves and to their men that they *are* highly sexual. And the men respond by getting it up as often as *they* can, as their way of proving that they are equal to the match. Both the men and the women are engaged in a not-so-subtle battle to prove that they are "good in bed." Not good for each other, just good in bed. They seek to fulfill an abstract ideal, not each other. And, consequently, they don't. They keep reaching for an empty image, and they keep missing each other.

All of this produces a hardness and a toughness in the attitudes of both men and women. It is not just that their bodies are stiff with tension for fear they will do something to reveal that they are not the "perfect partners" they have prepared themselves so carefully to portray. It is more than this. They toughen their emotions also. Secretly they know that they are playing a charade, and secretly they have contempt for anyone who plays it with them, for anyone who cannot see beyond their charade and its façade. So they become tough. Soon the image becomes worn onto their faces. Soon the doll's paint doesn't come off. The sad results can be seen in any singles bar: overweight jocks with hair transplants and toupées playing out the game with thirty-year-old "girls." There are no winners in this game. There are only varying degrees of loss. It is no wonder, then, that the men and women who play this game become so cynical and suspicious.

In the midst of such an unholy sexual war—fought in a true "Valley of the Dolls"—it becomes a little easier to see the importance of tenderness in male sexuality. If sex becomes a male proving ground, just as business and athletics have become, then there is literally no haven left and no rest for the weary. Sex is more than penetration, more than orgasm. It is also the skin's thrill and warmth in being touched. It is the touch of eyes beyond where hands can go.

The importance of touch to the human organism now is understood as a need just like food and shelter. It is the feeding of the heart. Children who receive a lot of affectionate touching are vibrant and glowing. Ashley Montagu tells us that a person deprived of all touch simply will not live. Children who miss the vital nourishment of enough touching often grow up with a hunted, haunted expression on their faces. They think they want sex. What they want is a gentle touch. So they go through the sexual charade, knowing that at some point in the sexual dance the dancers both will touch.

If men could see their need for simple affection, and accept the deeply satisfying pleasure that gentleness and tenderness can provide, sex would cease to be a torture for them and might become a source of genuine growth. But that may be a lot to ask of men who are convinced that they have to be Burt Reynolds in order to be anyone at all.

The Difference Between Loving and Making Love

In an earlier book, *It's Me and I'm Here!** I described the difference between loving and making love. For many people, particularly the macho, this is a very slim difference indeed.

*Harold C. Lyon, Jr., *It's Me and I'm Here!* (New York: Delacorte Press, 1974).

Making love is largely a physical and intellectual experience, and at its best, when shared with someone you care about, it's not a "bad" thing, even occasionally for lovers. Loving, on the other hand, has added to it another dimension—the emotional component—and, at *its* best, a fourth dimension—the spiritual component. The difference between loving and making love is difficult to describe in words. Loving defies description. It has a here-and-nowness, a spontaneity to it, which can make it a tender and vulnerable experience. Loving has far more potential for fulfillment than making love.

When I use a rote approach to sexuality—a fixed set of learned responses, as in the clinical marriage manual, with fore-play, positions, and various prearranged techniques—I am usually only making love and I limit my potential severely. Making love is largely an experience of the head and body, with the emotions and spirituality largely denied. The word "making" in "making love" accurately labels the difference. In loving, there is no need for "making," since it all flows naturally.

The tough person is much more apt to be into "making" love, since such a person is usually physically and/or intellectu-ally oriented, and is underdeveloped spiritually and emotion-ally. The emotional domain and most certainly the spiritual component of the whole person are left out of most love-"mak-ing"—keeping sex from being a totally integrated process. It is more of a mechanical act than a human experience.

A machine just works; it doesn't feel. Many men, in their great desire to self-actualize their images instead of actualizing themselves, are given to performing like machines, with the emphasis on performance rather than on feeling or flowing. It is ironic that the treatment for one of the leading sexual com-plaints among men, premature ejaculation, is the application of a de-sensitizing ointment to the penis so that it will feel less to perform better. It is also ironic that the other most often mentioned sexual problem among men, impotence, is usually a result of trying to force oneself to *perform* better sexually—"making" again, not flowing. The truth is that the penis is not a mechanized attachment but an integral part of the male body. The noble penis cannot be forced or made to perform or obey commands of the head, even if we have stooped so low as to force ourselves into such a subservient role. And so we drug the penis with anesthetizing ointments so it will not naturally feel and have "sense" to follow what is natural for it.

The overly toughened male today is fearful of his potency, and hence is afraid of involvement on an intimate level. This anxiety manifests itself in an overexaggerated "coolness" or suaveness about sexual matters which only diminishes passion and tenderness. To treat mechanically a relationship as beautiful and tender as the sexual one is to see "liberated men and women" treating each other more like accessories than human beings. Rollo May, in his excellent book *Love and Will,* cites *Playboy* magazine and its "cool" approach to sex as an example of this phenomenon. Speaking of the nude centerfold girls he says:

As you look more closely you see a strange expression in these photographed girls: detached, mechanical, uninviting, vacuous—the typical schizoid personality. . . . you discover that they are not 'sexy' at all, but that *Playboy* has only shifted the fig leaf from the genitals to the face.*

Total Orgasm Versus Partial Ejaculation

A lot has been written on the orgasm in the past few years. One would think it to be the most ardently sought after goal of modern man and woman. Many of us probably have heard more about techniques for achieving orgasm than we ever

*Rollo May, *Love and Will* (New York, Norton, 1969) p. 57.

needed or wanted to know. For the tender person, orgasm is not the goal of everything in his or her sexual experience. Sharing feelings, fantasies, and the inner spiritual richness, which often takes time—this is the full process of sexual communication that enables the physical to transcend itself to the emotional, and the emotional to transcend itself to the spiritual. This is loving as compared to making love. Yet we treat orgasm as a final end to which any means is justifiable.

The quality of orgasm and the afterglow flowing from it for a person in touch with his or her tenderness is vastly different from the jerky mechanical ejaculation or climax of a person heavily armored by toughness. When one is toughened—subconsciously fighting orgasm while consciously fighting to achieve it at all costs (rather than flowing tenderly into it and through it and beyond it by letting go and surrendering totally to it)—all the muscles tighten and it becomes a painful and almost cramping experience, the sounds of which testify to the quality of the episode.

Many people sound as though they are having a leg amputated without anesthesia during their orgasms, or as if they are lifting a thousand-pound weight off their foot. Love sounds are a natural and beautiful "music," but groans that express more pain than joy reveal only the rigidity of a person's body and emotions. A person who is aware of his own tenderness as well as his partner's can flow through orgasm with sounds and cries that are testimonials to his pleasure and joy.

I am distinguishing between orgasm (for both males and females) and ejaculation (for the male) or climax (for the female). An orgasm, as I am defining it, is the integrated experience of the whole person. An ejaculation or climax is a localized genital experience of the tough or controlled person. An orgasm, from my experience, spreads outwardly from the genitals through the entire abdomen and even out to the extremities

. . . and on out toward infinity on rare occasions. One literally lets go of all the holding back emotionally, physically, intellectually, and spiritually. This is not an easy thing to do for most of us after having so many taboos laid over our sexuality from childhood on. It is a very vulnerable act to surrender so entirely to the blending of our own rhythms. Often it takes some therapy to thaw out and disarm people's defenses enough to free the tenderness within them which will allow their orgasms to flow rather than to "make" themselves or their partners "come."

The damage done by many marriage manuals is widespread. The male is told that he must "perform" and hold back his ejaculation until the inevitably "slower" female reaches her "more difficult to achieve" climax. He is even given advice on how to concentrate on other distractions such as office work or finances to numb his feelings and delay his ejaculation. Certainly the problems of premature ejaculation and impotence in the male and the difficulty of achieving climax in some women are complex. However, these disorders are largely the result of the vast alienation in our society and the numbness of individuals who are crying out for more intimacy while at the same time refusing to experience it. An excellent book for women on this subject has been written by Betty Dodson, *Liberating Masturbation.* Now we need one for men.

If the man will flow with his own rhythms, rather than attempt to perform or achieve for his mate, both he and his partner may find themselves amazed at the results. Often a woman following her man's flow toward and through his own orgasm will, if her man is truly flowing and not merely performing, find herself thrust to the edge of her own orgasm, which will erupt from within her naturally. The greater the surrender, the greater the eruption.

A few years ago I became aware of a real deception in my own sexuality. I suspect I may not be alone in this, so I mention it here. What I discovered was that at the moment of orgasm I would attempt to emit deep bass-sounding groans—instead of the tender, uncontrolled cries which would naturally come from within me. I realized that for years I had been shifting from these natural falsetto cries to the more "masculine"-sounding gasps. I realized that I had been afraid that my partner would think of me as a boy and not a man if my love cries sounded childlike. How incredible! Even at the moment of release, to be so controlled.

Now I have reacquired my original impulse. I am more able to flow and become and sound like whoever I am during sex, be it boy-child-man-animal, or whatever. This has given me another way to hear who I am, and another way to speak.

Even in the unlikely arena of pornographic filmmaking, the need for tenderness is becoming apparent. Tina Russell, a friend of mine who is familiar with this business, tells me that there is a movement afoot to attempt to capture the full erotic impact of sexual loving rather than the usual rehearsed "ecstasies." That porno film would be rare—and successful—if it were able to capture the beauty of a tender hero and heroine in what I am calling total orgasm. Such a film would be truly erotic.

Experiments in Sexual Tenderness

If you doubt what I am saying, try doing the following experiment. Sometime when you and your partner both feel free enough to do this, tape-record your own love sounds. Compare what you hear to what you may hear in any porno film. My wife and I did this, and we were amazed at the beauty and power of our own love music. It was far more erotic and pure than anything we had ever heard or seen. Attempting this experiment can prove to you and your partner that you actually are the stars in your own private "T" for tender rated movie—a drama far more exquisite and exciting than any of the X-rated films.

I do not feel that pornography is "bad." But it deludes people. It has a clinical, unnatural, purely physical orientation devoid of much of the emotion, and certainly the spirituality, of true loving. Pornography for those people with few sexual outlets is probably better than no outlet at all, and I am in favor of its availability for consenting adults. But it cannot approach the sense of release and fulfillment that real loving offers. It is a safe way for a person to encounter sex totally removed from any emotional tie or relationship with others. Sensitively made pornography can be a spicy variant in the sexual menus of free lovers, but it is hardly what we would choose as a steady diet. It just isn't nourishing enough. There is no touch in it, no passion, no contact.

In porno films you can observe the tight faces of the male stars. Many of them have such controlled ejaculations that their frozen faces and bodies betray little sign or sound of what is occurring. This is "coolness" of the most severe order: a trait which seems to be much emulated in our age of alienation. I associate "coolness" with coldness and with deadness. A climax for a "cool" person is usually limited in feeling and sensation to the genital area. Psychologists and sex researchers report that such men simply do not realize that orgasm is a total-body event. In a complete orgasm, the entire body lets go. The whole being is involved, not only the body, let alone merely the sexual organ. Yet many men cheat themselves of this experience.

Likewise, the man who tries too hard to *get* hard is likely not to stay hard. The macho who strives to meet some impossible ideal of potency is fooling himself. And the body defies such commands. Head cannot dictate orders blindly. Often impotence is really the body's mutiny. Our genitals are among our tenderest organs, physically as well as psychologically. They are not "its"; they are intimate parts of our body and being. They are really doors to intimacy and oceanic feelings—if we will surrender to the flow within us that leads us to these doors.

Regaining Sexual Innocence

Innocence is that freedom from guilt which we all enjoyed during early childhood. Then nothing was "bad" or "wrong." Life was alive then, not quantified and categorized. This kind of innocence is important in releasing and communicating our total sexuality.

The macho male, unfortunately, has become so "tough" that he is usually remote from the spontaneity and aliveness of innocence. In childhood our sexual feelings and desires were innocent until we were chastised or punished for expressing them. An experiment which can help us regain our sexual tenderness and innocence is to relive some of our childhood sexual fantasies and then replay little boy-girl games with someone for whom we care a great deal and with whom we are willing to explore these fantasies. These games can be played almost anywhere, but secluded natural environments are ideal. Share with your partner several childhood experiences or fantasies and pick out one that you both agree you'd like to relive. Concentrate on getting into your childhood space and feelings of innocence, letting go of all the need to perform or be protected or grown up.

Place yourselves several yards apart from each other—far enough so you can "see" or "grok" with "soft eyes." Become aware of your inhibitions and blocks, breathe deeply, and see if you can let go of the holding back bit by bit. Savor the visual delights of your partner, let your eyes roam freely all over his or her body, but keep coming back to the eyes to share. It is through this deep eye contact that the natural flow of spiritual feelings can be released as you become aware of who is really there in the other, and in you.

The power which can flow through such surrendering is truly boundless. There are orgasms which happen in the eyes, too. Try this simple exercise and *see* for yourself.

When I was a teenager, during a period when my father was stationed in Germany, I created a whole fantasy life out of my own sexual innocence. In the beautiful German forests, I would occasionally find an idyllic setting in the deep woods where a beam of sunlight would illumine a moss-covered "stage." There, with nature for my audience, I would undress and dance through the forest naked like the god Pan. My free and tender rompings would be consummated by the deepest of orgasms as I fantasized that behind a nearby tree a young wood nymph was watching me and was overcome at the purity of my eroticism.

At some point during my adolescence, I became quite guilty and ashamed about my unusual love affair with nature. I felt that I must be insane or "abnormal." Many years later, during the process of psychotherapy, I grew to accept my far-out ways and even learned to see in them the beauty of unforced, creative erotic energy.

Probably the most innocent experience of all is simply to be held at a mother's breast. Few of us receive enough of this basic intimacy, which may be why few of us feel comfortable with intimacy as adults. It is hard to hold on to the macho pose while at the breast of one you love. It is possible to re-create this intimacy. When a man and his mate feel ready—and particularly when the man is willing to let go of his I-can-do-it-all-by-myself pose—he can become an infant at his lover's bosom. He can be cradled in her arms and surrender.

This simple experiment can be extremely powerful for both the man and the woman. Why does extreme pleasure seem so difficult to accept? Why does it seem "wrong"? What can be wrong about innocence?

Unconventional as it may seem, there is no reason why two close women friends cannot also share this experience. Why should a woman be prohibited from re-experiencing this innocent intimacy? There is no good reason. To deprive women of this closeness simply because of society's "shoulds" and "should-nots" is only to reinforce the stereotypes we all need to move beyond. At the breast we are all equal.

Another way I have found to open myself is simply to kiss and be kissed on the eyelids. There is something so vulnerable and so caring in this gesture. It goes far beyond words of explanation. Open yourself. Close your eyes. Feel the kiss of someone you love enter your being and become part of your own love.

Massage: Learning to Rub People the Right Way

Another way to release your inherent tenderness is through massage. Here you can often invent your own best experiments yourself. Massage offers us all a way to give each other the love and stroking we need. Touch is food for the skin, the primary organ by which we contact our world. Few if any of us have experienced enough gentle touch. Massage is an excellent way for us to give and to get. We can all learn to be softer.

The important thing in massage is the tenderness of touching and being touched. Frequently, the most important thing in a sexual experience is that it provides an opportunity for intimate touching rather than the sexual activity in itself. Massage also gives us this slow, sensuous touching we all need. I'm referring to so-called Esalen-type massage, named for its advent at the Esalen Institute in Big Sur, California, rather than the thumping, slapping, meat-tenderizing variety popular in locker rooms and gyms, or the 42nd Street craze, the neon-lit massage parlors where for twenty dollars the female attendant will relieve a man of his sexual tension by giving a "local" hand job. It's a telling commentary on our society that we are so "out of touch," and so desperate for touch, that these parlors are doing a thriving business in spite of their lack of intimacy. However, in my opinion, we are better off with them than with nothing, as they at least provide a surrogate touching experience for those who so badly need it and who, without it, might display even more desperate behavior to get the touch they need.

The Esalen massage is a sensuous, tender massage. The hands of the massager move away from one's body gently and slowly, letting the person being massaged know that the hands are not rejecting or leaving the person, but that they will return for more stroking, touching, and tenderness.

I received my first Esalen massage some years ago at the Esalen Institute on the cliffs where the hot sulphur baths overlook the ocean at Big Sur. Gabrielle, my masseuse, met me in the baths, where I had been soaking for an hour. Experiencing the gentleness of this beautiful woman was a rare experience for the macho male I was in those days. In a secluded room with the sound of the ocean our only background noise, she knelt naked beside me with her fingertips extended, lightly resting them on my stomach as I lay on my back on the massage table. She instructed me in a gentle voice to flow and go wherever I would, and to relax and surrender to the full experience of my own feelings. With eyes closed, she meditated for five or ten minutes until she communicated with me, female to male. I worried about sexual feelings—a fear of having an erection from her touch. But she began to dispel my worries by systematically and tenderly massaging each of my muscle groups, telling me not to worry about sexual feelings, to go beyond them into the spiritual, that all my feelings were acceptable and good. After massaging each separate muscle group with coconut oil, she then integrated them all with long strokes which went from foot to thigh, to buttocks, to back, to neck, shoulders, arms, and hands. It was the most glorious experience I could recall ever receiving, and all by a lovely stranger. I had been starved for touch and "out of touch" with my own body, which now tingled and glowed with a new life I hadn't experienced since my childhood years.

Try it. All you need is leisure time, a comfortable place without interruptions, a willing partner, a little oil, and your own tenderness for several hours of this most pleasurable pastime. There are several excellent books now on the market which can guide you to the art of massage.

Experimenting with tenderness in sexuality can be helpful in indicating where you need more work in thawing out your body armor. Further, when it is integrated with your other therapeutic growth work, this experimenting can help you open yourself to more natural and tender sexual flow with your partner.

It is not my intention to treat sexuality in an oversimplified way. Sex is both a delicate and volatile aspect of our nature, one fraught with great complexity. It is the oversimplified treating of sexual matters as isolated skills that must be learned like riding a bicycle or swimming that deludes the macho male. The experiments I have presented here are not offered as instant exercises leading to tenderness in sexuality, but rather as catalytic steps toward getting in touch with the inherent tender core of us that has been buried beneath our encrusted outer shells. I find a great deal of my creativity bound up in my erotic energies. These exercises in tenderness help to unlock the flow in me.

The person who is able to regain his or her tenderness will be able to flow not only sexually, but in relationships of all kinds with other human beings. The great rewards of being in touch with your tenderness will come naturally to you as you work and grow in your own ways. The lines between tenderness in sexual flow and tenderness in other relating will begin to disappear as you become more integrated. The macho male tends to compartmentalize sex away from other aspects of his life, when sex can be a vital aspect of all the experiences of life. The mechanical aspects of sexuality will disappear for us as we begin to allow our erotic awareness its free rein. We can then realize, as Rollo May suggests, the real differences between a limited concept of sex and the true multidimensionality and globalness of Eros. Eros permeates many aspects of our lives. Eros is energy for living.

Eros takes wings from human imagination and is forever transcending all techniques, giving the laugh to all the "how to" books by gaily swinging into orbit above our mechanical rules, making love rather than manipulating organs. . . . It is this urge for union with the partner that is the occasion for human tenderness. For Eros—not sex as such —is the source of tenderness.*

A Shared Vision of Surrender

One morning, I got up alone at five A.M. to troll for lake trout on Lake Winnipesaukee, where I was vacationing and writing during my annual month of renewal. For the previous ten days I had been trolling a hundred feet down in the cold depths where the lake trout remain in August. That morning the fishing was in vain. At five forty-six the sun began putting on a spectacular display, painting the sky with feathers of golden oranges and reds. I had been using a pearl wobbler, which had been successful the year before. I was trolling at the right speed and in the right place. All my techniques were perfect. Now it was up to the trout. For three hours I trolled through the old spots with no success at all, until when I was

*Rollo May, *Love and Will*, pp. 73–74.

about to head back to the dock suddenly I had a heavy strike. I knew it must be a large fish by the way it tore line off my reel even with a heavy drag on it.

With one hand I reached down and turned off the motor, to stop my forward movement and to blend better with the morning quiet of the lake and the large trout that was hooked to my line somewhere down in the clear depths of the lake. Twenty minutes later, when I finally got her close enough to see the boat, she sounded in one last deep run for freedom. The hook held, and with one hand weary and holding the rod high, I finally slipped the landing net under the now tired monster trout and raised her out of the water and into the boat.

What a beautiful creature! The trout's spots were bright pink against the dark golden body, and her fat belly was pure white in the early morning sun. A precious moment to savor! Later, on the dock, my hands all bloody from cleaning my twenty-six-inch prize, I found her full of red roe. I washed from my hands the sweet subtle smell of fresh lake fish—so different from the overwhelming pungency of saltwater fish—and tiptoed back up to the cottage and into bed where my wife slept, and I shared with her my joy in finally catching a big trout.

We had not been comfortable in our relationship for the past few months, struggling to resolve our differences and blaming each other for them. How silly. How useless. Our lovemaking had become mechanical, lacking the flow and fulfillment we both sought. An hour after I had climbed back into bed, we found ourselves making love with incredible passion, spontaneity, and tender joy, flowing from orgasm to orgasm. There was a letting go, a total surrendering to our own inner rhythms, which had eluded us for months. In the midst of my orgasm I had a vision of the big lake trout, organic and beautiful in the depths of the lake, and I realized that I could not *make* her take my lure even when it was presented with perfect technique.

She had to be ready to strike the lure, with no holding back. This was a natural flowing instinct, not something I could force or manipulate.

Incredibly, in the afterglow of our loving, Eta shared with me that she too had seen a vision of the organic lake trout in the throes of *her* orgasms! We both realized in a flash that with all the technique in the world, we couldn't make our love flow until it was ready to flow, any more than I could make the lake trout take the lure. The taking of the lure down in the depths —like the surrendering to our deep feelings and flow—had to be total, without holding back and protecting. We two had fused into one for a few precious moments, sharing a spiritual insight in our joint vision of the lake trout, and it had helped us to regain our love at a deeper level.

Later, as we lay together, two of the children knocked on our bedroom door with a surprise. Breakfast in bed! It was as though the love vibrations had passed from us through the entire house. Somehow, they knew.

The feelings my wife and I shared through this experience are well expressed in a poem written by my friend Gabriel Heilig, which appropriately enough he calls "Lovescape."*

> Again, again, I meet your soul in mine,
>   and join the full moon in its flight.
> The world's bright body moves between,
>
> first white, then brown, then Life's deep jade design,
>   then ruby-blazed, then rusted gold, then white
> again. Again, I meet your soul in mine,
>
> and feel the swirling ocean's spine
>   stir the smoking ebonies of night.
> The world's bright body moves between

---

*© 1977

us, the dawn in sequined orangedown,
   the hungry gulls each wheeling and await.
Again, again, I meet your soul in mine

to taste such simple peace as gods will deign
   to let flesh find. In their slowly smiling sight,
the world's bright body moves between

us now—the gleaming lightshafts hidden, slant and fine,
   as deep in the ribboning water spins the light.
Again, again, I meet your soul in mine.

   The world's bright body moves and moves between.

11 The Tenderness of Being a Father

Fatherhood: A Special Time of Growth

The father-child relationship, though often stereotyped as a kind of a rough-and-tumble tough affair, can be the most satisfying and tender relationship possible. When you contemplate that a father has been a part of his child's existence from the moment of conception on, fatherhood becomes what it is—a miracle.

Fatherhood is a time of special awareness. It is a time for us fathers to re-experience the child-consciousness in ourselves and to relive the beauty and innocence of youth with our children. As fathers, we become both man and child; we grow in both directions.

I feel that it is important for couples having children to plan on having the father's participation throughout the process of pregnancy, including his presence in the delivery room at the moment of birth. The father can play an active role throughout the pregnancy, being with the mother-to-be, encouraging and assisting her. Through the Lamaze and Bradley methods of natural birth, and the Leboyer "birth without violence" method, an active caring role for the father is an integral part of the total birth process. The father plays a crucial role as a partner, helping the mother with breathing exercises and in the actual delivery of the child. A tone of tenderness can be set and expressed from the earliest moments on, thereby establishing a pattern between father and child. By participating actively in this event, the father can become a full partner in the parenting relationship.

Yet for many men fatherhood seems to be a burden. They see it as an additional responsibility (which it surely is) rather than as an incredible source of nourishment and joy. In a magazine interview, the actor Dustin Hoffman put it very well, saying that he had never realized how much joy and aliveness could be communicated simply through a child's smile. When that child is your own, the joy can be overwhelming. And it is free, given purely out of the joy your child feels within its own heart.

Many men will not surrender to this joy in their children. They will not just let their children be who they are. They feel a need to turn them into something else—a baseball player, a doctor, a soldier, a miniature version of all of their own unfulfilled fantasies. Children don't need their parents' fantasies. They need a continuity of experience and a continuity of caring. This gives them the strength and the space to explore *their own* fantasies, the ones they will have to learn to turn into actuality in their own lives.

There is a beautiful paradox in fatherhood. The more a father can surrender to his children, can leave his world and enter theirs, the more he can experience of their joy. He will be welcomed in the endless richness of the child's world, which is spun out of the sheer delight children feel in everything around them. They have no judgments. They have no expectations for themselves. They do not think of themselves in terms of whether they will go to college or be successful. They are already successful at being who they are. If a father wants to love his children, he can learn to participate with them *as they are.* The more strength and love he can give them, the easier it will be for them to make a smooth and natural transition into adulthood, when the time comes for that.

The irony of all this is that, in large part, being a successful father is simply a matter of being willing to let things go their own way and of allowing children the space to follow their own impulses within certain boundaries dictated by considerations of safety. There is not a lot a father has to do. Nature will assure that children will grow, given certain minimum conditions of health and nurture. Many fathers miss the ecstasy of playing with their children and re-entering the child's world because they are already bent on "making a success" of their son. Their son has his entire life to make a success of himself—but he gets his youth only once. Fathers can open to their children's need *to be children* and can participate with their children *as they are.* The more successfully the father can open the child within himself, the more communication he will have with his children. He will be able to experience their world as *they* do, and they will then be more willing to experience his, when the time comes for that transition. They will not view their father as an alien "adult," but as another person with whom they can share their experience.

Bedtime Stories

I have two sons. Until my divorce, I made it an almost sacred habit to spend a few minutes each night weaving for them a spontaneous bedtime adventure fantasy about two young brothers close in age to my two boys. For no special reason, many years ago the fictional boys took on the names of Buba and Jude. These two boys, through these stories, over the years, lived all the adventures and peak experiences which had happened to me as a child, plus others I invented.

As a child, I was actively linked with nature through my avid interest in wildlife of all varieties. Also, as the son of a traveling Army officer, I attended sixteen different schools around the world before ever beginning my higher education. The often traumatic adjustment to new and changing environments made life an ever-challenging adventure rather than an overwhelmingly oppressive experience for me. Accordingly, the adventures of Buba and Jude were largely stories of the adjustment of children to the exciting world of woodlore, wildlife, and other human beings.

During their bedtime stories my sons were always a captive audience; they seemed to have almost total recall of stories I had long since forgotten. I was frequently amazed at the detail they remembered. On occasions when creating a new story about Buba and Jude "heading across the potato patch and down the hill to the swamp, turning right toward the cave," I was interrupted by Eric or Gregg saying, "No, Daddy! You have to turn left, not right, to go to the cave!"

Though each story was different, told during the tranquillity that (usually) preceded bedtime, they were all consistent with respect to geographic detail and continuity. A map of the world of Buba and Jude became imprinted in the minds of my boys as they vicariously shared this adventurous world. They constructed a mental map with which they tied together the adventures and concepts which I wove into the stories.

Later, as a teacher, it occurred to me that if I could only tune in my students' receivers to bedtime-story attentiveness, I could really begin to approach maximum learning efficiency rather than the 5 to 10 percent efficiency normally achieved in the classroom. It then hit me that I had been a teacher, and that every parent is a teacher in the best sense of the word, when telling a bedtime story. What a great time to communicate the important concepts and values of life that far too often slip by so many families in the rush of modern society! I had woven into the adventures of Buba and Jude those concepts that I wanted to get across to my boys: concepts such as courage, honesty, chivalry, the golden rule, sharing, teamwork, and even sex education. I realize now that we are all teachers or students (and even these roles are interchangeable) most of our waking hours, and that the bedtime-story time is fertile ground in which to plant some seeds. As I have watched my boys grow, I have been able to see some of these seeds sprout and blossom.

Quite a few years later I sat down with my boys and we decided to write together a busy father's bedtime storybook, *The Adventures of Buba and Jude.* (They really wrote the book, because they remembered many more of the stories than I did.) The re-creating of these tales, which we dictated into a tape recorder, was a very precious experience to share with them. They reflected back to me so much of the love and caring I had attempted to give to them through these stories when they had been younger. Truly, nothing is ever lost.

The relationship between a father and his daughter has a poignancy all its own, and we are probably more apt to associate this relationship with tenderness than that between father and son. A boy's father is the most important role model that a youngster will ever have. It is crucial that it be a tender one if the child is to emerge with a sense of his own role in this often numbing world. Moments of tenderness communicated by a father probably have a greater significance and impact on a child than any later examples.

In school, alas, there are far too few male role models among the elementary teacher ranks. So bedtime offers a relaxed opportunity for the father to just *be there* with his children. This is a time to reflect on the day's activities, as eyelids begin to lower slowly and safely into sleep. The bedtime can become an important time for your child by providing a "sea anchor": a daily ritual which can quickly become part of your shared history. Every family needs these sea anchors to tug gently at the ship as they sail on with eyes focused on some new horizon.

When to stop telling bedtime stories? Never! You can tell them, not only to your children, but to those others with whom you have important relationships. No one is too old for such intimacy. Most of us remember being children snuggling in the love of a father's words. And some of us would love to be children again.

The Mourning Process in Divorce

I always have felt a very close bond with my two sons. Though I had weaknesses as a father (allowing my professional career to take me away from them often, bringing disruption into their early lives), I feel that my strongest asset was my ability to be tender and childlike with them—to "get off" the position of being a "serious adult," and to play mischievously with them.

When my first marriage ended in divorce, it was an excruciatingly painful time for me, particularly in regard to my separation from my sons. They were eight and nine years old, and they identified closely with me.

I realized then that divorce is in some ways more difficult for children to accept than the death of a parent. When a child's parent dies, there is a finality to it. Through the mourning process, the child is actually forced into facing much of the impact of the loss of the parent and how much that loss means. The mourning process is important in that the mourner very deeply experiences his *own* loneliness. Only by experiencing our own loneliness do we re-emerge with new vitality for living our lives without the lost loved one. In divorce, however, there is no finality to trigger the process of mourning. One of the two most important people in the child's world has left. Not forever, inasmuch as he is alive out there in the world somewhere, visiting occasionally, or sending money or presents, or writing letters. Father lives, but he is no longer "Father." Very often the child blames himself for this sudden separation. He cannot understand this complex event, and the other parent is often too upset emotionally to talk about it sensibly and in terms that a child can understand.

With over 40 percent of our marriages now ending in divorce, we parents need to learn to lead our children caringly through the mourning process when it occurs. In my own case I awkwardly and accidentally, though tenderly, stumbled through such a process with my two boys. It took me over a year to realize and to accept that I was actually no longer "Father" to my two sons—a role which was so important to me and to my self-concept.

This painful truth is most real for the parent who does not obtain custody of the children. Hard as we may try, there is no way to remain a full-time father when visiting only a few times a month. This is the painful truth which both parent and child must mourn—the loss of father and the loss of children. We fathers or mothers without custody must accept the fact that from now on we are more like visiting aunts or uncles or "friends" than we are fathers or mothers. This loss is severe for both parent and child.

I shared this realization with my two sons shortly after my separation from their mother. I let them know that I wanted very much to continue to be there with them, tucking them into bed each night, telling them bedtime stories, hunting and fishing together, but the truth was that I was not going to be able to be there with them day in and day out as their father.

I told them that I was their father and would always be, that we would share many special times together from time to time, and that it was a terrible loss for me also that I would not be there with them every day. I told them that it was not their fault, not their mother's, not mine—that at times two people just couldn't seem to work things out together without creating more hurt and pain than happiness, and that there was no one to blame for this misfortune. I felt my grief begin to surface from deep within me as I shared this lonely realization with them. I sobbed, and they shared this mourning experience with me. It was one of the most difficult but important experiences of my life. I know it helped the three of us re-emerge with new vitality for living our lives anew, though apart.

For the first year or two of our visitations I found myself attempting to make our visits into "perfect" superweekends. Since I was with them only one weekend a month plus one month in the summer, I wanted their times to be memorable. It became an incredible strain, not only for me, but for them as well. And this is a mistake many divorced fathers make. I discovered that my boys really enjoyed a relaxed and natural easy-paced weekend around the house, more than my carefully staged Saturday circus, Sunday fishing-and-hiking-trip, spectacular weekend specials. The natural time provided more space for us to share ourselves with one another. The boys began to choose how to spend these visits.

Often they chose to "do" nothing. We just hung out together. The specific events were less important than the experience of *being* with one another. Trying to make up for lost time on his visitations, a father tends to create a tough act for the mother to follow when he leaves the boys off, tired and dirty after their exciting foray. Just as it's easy to show your best side in a short-term relationship, as compared to the long-term marriage relationship, so it's also temptingly easy to appear to be the perfect loving parent on a once-a-month weekend visit—leaving someone else to be the everyday parent responsible for discipline and the other natural but often unpleasant tasks of making a household function well. And I wondered why my ex-wife's resentments still smoldered long after our divorce!

One of the biggest disappointments I have had to face in my life has been my own personal failure as a father. It is literally impossible for the parent without custody to be a truly successful parent. This is not to suggest that we should give up doing all we can. But it is important to have realistic expectations, which initially I did not. It is one thing to do all we can as the ones who have fathered our children and who love and care for them dearly; but to hold on to the fantasy that we can still be everyday fathers *in absentia* is unrealistic. As long as we hold on to that fantasy, we will always fall short of our hopes and never understand why. As soon as we can accept what our role is realistically—somewhere short of the "ideal" father—then we will begin enjoying what we *are* able to do, and so will our children.

The Father as a Sole Parent: Some Fathers' Personal Statements on Nurturing

Many fathers have had to face up to the issue of their role as a sole parent. Does a father possess the tenderness and nurturance for such a role? Our legal organizations and our courts traditionally have not thought so. Behind the traditional ruling that the mother shall have custody is the notion that only she has the tenderness, the nurturing ability, and the time (since she is still often not thought of as the "breadwinner") to properly care for and rear children. Groups of fathers have organized nationally and locally in an organization called "Fathers United for Equal Rights" in an effort to undo some of the injustice which exists in our legal system of divorce rulings. This organization has helped fathers gain custody of their children by stressing to the courts, and in the media, that a father need not lack the tenderness needed to be a sole parent. The notion that only mothers can be tender is certainly a fallacy. I have been interested in talking with fathers who have become sole parents to ascertain their own notions and feelings about their tenderness.

What follows are personal statements of several courageous fathers who have struggled against the prevailing social norm that only mothers should rear their children. They portray these fathers' notions of their own struggles to give their children what they need.

TENDERNESS TOWARD A CHILD'S SOUL

by Robert Gary

Our family broke up about two years ago. Since then, my fourteen-year-old son and I have lived by ourselves. My daughter lives with her mother. There were no disagreements about custody. We pretty much let the children decide which parent they wanted to live with.

On many mornings, my son's day begins when I wake him by rubbing his back. It's a chance to give some physical contact in a way that's not uncomfortable for either of us. We still kiss goodnight—it's kind of a salute on the cheek—but this is becoming less frequent. I try to be sensitive to his level of comfort with these physical interchanges, and increase them or decrease them according to his signs of need or embarrassment. Being sensitive to his level of need is a kind of tenderness in itself, and I think he appreciates it. It gives him room to grow away from me at his own rate.

I've never thought much about tenderness before. It doesn't bother me to be spoken of as tender. I know it's an important quality for me to have in rearing my son. He is the most important person in my life right now. And I hope he will absorb the quality of tenderness into his own personality. I'd like him to be a tender father someday.

I think there are two kinds of tenderness. One is the physical kind, as when a parent snuggles with an infant and soothes a hurt. My former wife was one of the most tender women I've ever known. It was instinctive to her. And I am glad that my children experienced it when they were very young.

I am not as tender physically as I would like to be. I'm improving, but it would be difficult to equal the physical tenderness that my former wife was capable of. I think the reason is that I saw little physical tenderness in my own parents.

There is another kind of tenderness, however, that shows in the way a parent handles a child's soul. It says to a child that he is a person in his own right, one whose feelings deserve a response and a respect. That kind comes easy and natural to me. I had it from my parents, it's part of my being, and I hope to pass it on to my children. My son has learned it already. He is tender to me, considerate, respectful of my moods and needs—and I love him for it. I often see him deal with others the same way. Because of this, he will never have trouble getting along with people. He will always be secure emotionally.

TENDERNESS IN BEING A FATHER: SOME THOUGHTS AND EXPERIENCES

by Dick Orth

Being tender as a father has been a moving and growing experience for me. My ability to be tender, particularly as a father, has grown;

or more accurately, has had to grow, at least as fast as my three sons have grown. They are now sixteen, thirteen, and nine.

When Rick, the oldest, was born I was a lieutenant in the Army —airborne, ranger, tough and demanding. I was really proud to have a son for a first child. Since he was a baby, cute, cuddly and playful, it was easy for me to be tender with him. Even hard-nosed rangers are moved by toddlers as they learn to walk, throw a ball, talk and respond to hugging. It was very safe and acceptable to me to hug, kiss, and hold this young baby boy to whom I would teach all my skills and knowledge about being a man.

When he was about three, I decided he was old enough to learn to ski. Never mind that it was near zero in one of the coldest winters in recent German history; I was going to teach him this skill—and he damned well would learn. I had seen kids of six schussing the slopes and my son would be one of them. Besides, braving the cold and snow was learning to be manly in the best soldierly tradition.

We lasted about an hour on the hill behind our quarters. As he fell repeatedly in the snow, I tenderly brushed him off, warmed his hands between mine, and reassured him that it "really wasn't too cold out." As he continued to cry, it really was my susceptibility to the softer feelings of love and compassion that called a halt to the agony—both his and mine. I had an awareness of tenderness but it was buried under a thick layer of what I thought it meant to be manly.

But the tenderness was there. As he grew older and it became clearer that his interest in athletic accomplishment didn't match my drive, it was the tenderness I had to get in touch with on a more regular basis. Here was an exciting little boy, who was clever at stringing cable cars on blocks and twine all around his bedroom, and who loved stories and make-believe. He didn't have my interest in sports. By opening myself to my tenderness, or at least by not resisting it, I moved beyond my frustration and pain. Then I could love him for who he was, instead of who I thought he should be. Some loving (and sometimes not too indirect) reminders from my wife about my own feelings of inadequacy helped a bit. The fact that Rick's interest in soldiers and the military goes way beyond mine also helped. Now, when his long discussions of uniforms and tactics from the Seven Years' War cause me to think that my son is a reincarnation of Frederick the Great, our ability to hug each other, cry, and share our pain keeps our relationship vibrant.

More and more it seems to me that the experience of being the father of three sons calls for continual tenderness, rather than authority. Unless I'm willing to be tender and vulnerable when dealing with the boys, communication of our deeper feelings, hopes, and dreams doesn't take place. If I fall into my order-giving pattern, which is easy for me to do, especially when I'm tired, I'm quickly tuned out. Not only is my physical presence necessary to get them to do what I want, but the whole experience becomes one of two robots making noise. When I can say something like "I really need your help," they respond quicker and we can go on and share more deeply with each other.

I see tenderness as being willing to get beyond my judgments, advice, and opinions and risk the consequences of sharing my feelings. When I'm willing to do that, the boys are, too. Then there can be open expressions of love and mutual support.

Recently, in one of my fits of anger at all the boys, I ended my tirade with "Be careful, because I'm a mean old son of a bitch!" Paul, completely unbothered, just turned and said, "That's not true and you know it." He blew my act completely, so I opened myself again to the joy and pain of living.

DISCIPLINE AS TENDERNESS

by Leonard Grossman

We were finishing dinner, the three of us—my five-year-old son, Scott, my six-and-a-half-year-old daughter, Jody, and I—and were having dessert—canned peaches, I recall. After that was consumed my daughter asked, "Can I have some ice cream now?"

"O.K.," I said and served her. She proceeded to polish off the ice cream and decided she wanted some rock candy to complete the meal. Since I felt I had to be both father and mother to the child, since her mother had left us the year before, and not wanting to deny her anything, I permitted it. She then trotted off to the living room with a full belly to watch television.

A half hour later she appeared before me looking genuinely unhappy. "Daddy, my stomach hurts," she told me. "That's because you had so many desserts," I said. She looked at me. "Why did you let me?" she asked.

This was another lesson in the intensive continuing course I was getting from my children in how to be a parent. I learned that being a pal wasn't what they wanted from me—they wanted leadership. They wanted a parent to guide them, to show them what was right and what was wrong, what was safe and what was dangerous and how dangerous; they wanted to have fun, yes, but they also sought information—a pilot to steer them through childhood.

About two years later the phone rang at my office. It was Jody's teacher at school. "Mr. Grossman, Jody asked me to call you. She has lost her dental appliance at lunch today and was afraid to wait until tonight to let you know."

Jody had been fitted with a removable brace for her teeth which she was supposed to wear at all times except when eating or brushing her teeth. Something must have distracted her in the school cafeteria and she had forgotten to replace it after eating lunch. Whoever had cleaned the tables must have thrown it out. When I got home that night I found a thoroughly frightened little girl. She was aware that dental appliances were expensive and that the loss was serious.

"What are you going to do to me?" she wanted to know. I had to think fast. She was expecting punishment. I hadn't thought about that, since I was so relieved that the teacher's phone call hadn't been about an injury or worse. But she expected punishment.

What could I do to "punish" her without hurting her but still let her believe that she was paying for her negligence? I tried to second-guess her. "You're confined to your room for one week. After you get home from school go straight to your room and stay there," I said. She seemed happy to hear that and began making preparations for the incarceration. She gathered coloring books, crayons, games, and other toys in her room so as to make the best of the situation. She did not resist the punishment and showed no animosity toward me. If anything, she indicated a deepened affection for me, as though the punishment were an expression of my love for her.

My kids have taught me that they want discipline. They want my companionship, and they like playing games in which they can include their father. We enjoy weekend trips together to nearby points of interest. They also like roughhousing and the body contact it affords. But they expect to pay for their lapses, even when they voice objection. I'm sure that permissiveness on my part would impart to them a feeling that I didn't care about them or that somehow I lacked something as a parent. I believe permissive parents delude themselves that they are ingratiating themselves with their kids. Children need to test their parents so that they can learn the limits of civilized behavior.

The parent who abdicates this responsibility may frustrate some children—and cause some others to grow up to be irresponsible misfits.

Jody and Scott have taught me that the best way to raise children is to enjoy them. No self-sacrifice is required. Occasionally when they try my patience—and this they do regularly—I'll ask them, "Do you want an angry daddy or a happy daddy?" and they get the message. It works both ways. Tenderness is strength, and conversely, surprisingly, strength is tenderness.

My Father: A Tender Man for a Role Model

I was fortunate to be blessed with a father who, in spite of thirty years in a successful career as an Army officer, is an exceptionally tender man. As I reflect upon my childhood years and compare my father with the fathers of my friends and relatives, it is apparent to me now that he possessed rare qualities as a tender role model for me.

I realize now that as a teenager I was perhaps even more macho than he was. He always washed the dishes, and I would feel bad because he was doing what I felt was a demeaning task for the "man of the house." I even resolved at the age of fourteen that I wasn't going "to be dominated" that way when I married. (Instead I find myself, much to my own delight, cooking many of the meals for my present family.)

Throughout my career as a junior Army officer, senior officers who had served under my father would come to me to tell me what a wonderful man he was—how personal and understanding he had been with them. One colonel told me that my father was the most human "commander" he had ever had; he understood that Army men had families and needed time to be with them. This colonel confided in me that on one occasion he had had a major dispute with his wife and had broken down in tears before his commanding officer, my father—an "unthinkable act of emotion" on the part of a professional soldier. My father had embraced him and given him time off to work out the problem with his wife. The colonel told me that my father had set an example of tenderness for him which influenced his entire career as an Army officer.

My father told me before I set out on my career as an Army officer, "Always take care of your men. If you do that, they will respect and care for you and go the extra mile often needed for success or survival." He also told me that when he was in the field with his regiment he never ate a bite of his food until he personally saw to it that all his troops had been fed.

This was quite a role model for me as a young lieutenant, and it influenced me greatly. When I took over the command of a combat-ready company of paratroopers in the 101st Airborne Division, I was warned by the departing commander to be stern with them because they were "a bunch of criminals who will try to get away with everything they can." Yet just the opposite approach—my father's way of treating the men as unique human beings—worked to make our company one of the best in the division.

Recently I watched my father with my own children when he joined us for a summer vacation of fishing and camping. His tenderness and love were obvious to us all. I am fortunate that he is a tender man and that the strength of his tenderness was given to me and passed on to my children. Our role models are so important to us. Unfortunately, there are few models of the tender father. Our society rewards heroes, not humanists, yet it is the humanists who keep us human in the end. Loving and being tender require a special courage of their own, and they give children the strength they will need to take their own forward steps toward loving and sharing later on in life. We may not all be in a position to be heroes, but we are all in a position to be warm and nurturing. That is what being a father is all about.

Beyond the Big-Shot Image

Fatherhood is more than lecturing at children. It means being willing to be more than a tough big-shot father. Big-shot fathers can be seen every weekend yelling at their sons on the Little League diamond, telling them how to do all the things they were never able to do themselves. These fathers are not being fair to their children. They are treating them in a way they would not want to be treated themselves. They are expecting adult skills from children. Real athletes know better. They are patient, because they know how much work and encouragement it took for *them* to make it as athletes. Big-shot fathers seem to care less about their children than they do about the well-being of their own egos. Their children quickly get the message and learn to tune their fathers out when they begin their Casey Stengel or Vince Lombardi act.

When a tough father senses that he is being tuned out, he often becomes enraged and yells even louder. It is a vicious cycle, leading downward in a negative spiral of noncommunication. His toughness becomes a barrier to his communication with his children—not the object lesson of manliness he may imagine it to be.

But tenderness is not simply a matter of not yelling. There are times when a good stern lecture or even a loud angry voice is the most honest way for a father to communicate with his children. Children know when adults mean what they say, and when they don't. Tenderness is primarily the willingness and the ability to flow with the here-and-now moment of the experience a father and his children are sharing. If it is a happy moment, there should be no hesitation by the father to let his "manly" defenses down and laugh gleefully with his children, enjoying their happiness with them. By the same token, he should also be willing to vent his anger when the occasion arises —not by exaggerating it or by dumping it all over his children, who are less able than he is to defend themselves from it, but simply by letting them know that he *is* angry.

A father who is willing to flow with his responses as he interacts with his children will find that they soon become much more able to "read" his emotions, and that his children lose their fear of being emotional. *Children acquire this fear from adults.* By taking the risk of being openly emotional with his children—crying at sad events, bubbling at happy ones, being afraid with them when he feels fear, and angry when he feels anger—a father can do a great deal to insure that his children will not grow up to be emotional cripples. Men who feel that they have to be "tough" all the time often find out, too late, that their children have become emotional zombies. They are not sensitive to their own emotional cues, or to those of other people. And since emotions are internal signaling devices to tell us how we feel about certain situations, the children of these "tough" men will actually be at a serious disadvantage in life. They will not know how they feel about things. And as a result they will more easily get themselves into situations which do not serve them, simply because they did not react honestly to them in the first place.

Emotional honesty is a form of tenderness. It is being willing to be the way you are, rather than the way you suppose you "should" be. So many fathers try to live out an imagined hero role for their children. This is particularly true of father-son relationships. Father-daughter relationships are often characterized by an emotional remoteness, as these "heroes" don't know how to be human with their little girl-children. They can't let go of their toughness to enter the natural courtesy and charm of a little girl's world. They think of it all as sissy stuff perhaps. As a result they turn their daughters into fearful young women who are constantly afraid they will displease Daddy. These are often the same girls who, in rebellion, run away from home or "get into trouble" at the first opportunity they find. No one likes to be dominated by anyone else, whether a father or a stranger. If fathers would understand that, they might enjoy a lot more warmth and welcome from their own children.

Second-Chance Families: Stepfatherhood

Fortunately for my boys, they have acquired a stepfather, really a new "father" (I find that difficult to say), someone who can provide on a day-to-day basis what I am not there to provide. I am also able to provide some things that I could not if I were there with them. For instance, I now offer them a new family of stepbrothers, stepsisters, and a stepmother from whom they have gained much and with whom they have enjoyed sharing many enjoyable adventures in living. They now have the not-to-be-taken-lightly advantage of two families, as well as the sometimes more confusing but broadening aspects of two value systems and life styles.

Additionally, I now have the opportunity to be a father again in a "second-chance family" with my stepchildren. Second marriages with children involved are far more complex than meets the eye. My wife, who plans to write a much-needed book on this subject, informs me that when all nine of us get together, as we sometimes do for holidays, some sixty-four separate relationships are being negotiated—each of us with each of the other eight! This creates enough energy and potential confusion to blow the roof off. And when you consider the complexities of the other former spouses remarrying and perhaps having more children in their new marriages, as my wife's former husband has, the complexities become fearsome.

As each of the separate families becomes another new family, there is a blending of different value systems, traditions, and customs. For example, in our case I can remember the protests that arose from Eta's children at our first Christmas together when my two sons and I got out our traditional red and green velvet ribbon to adorn the tree, and our equally strong response to their tradition of stringing popcorn and cranberries. And this was only about decorating a tree.

It is vital for all of us to realize that when we are together we are a new and different family with certain new advantages (the pluses of big-family fun experiences for me and my two boys, since we had never experienced this before) and certain disadvantages (less time, attention, and space with parents). Being a stepparent is a big responsibility, but it can also become a rewarding new exploration in growth.

Admittedly I am aware that I have been slow in totally accepting this new father role. A cautious voice inside me warns, "The pain of the first experience through divorce of not being able to be the kind of father you wanted to be with your two boys keeps you cautious about risking the full responsibility of trying again to be father to new stepchildren." It's another maze where doors have been slammed for me and painful memories linger. But there is also another voice, saying, "Fatherhood can be a special joy for you—if you take the risks. Take the risks!"

In summary, then, toughness in fatherhood results in a shallow and weak bond between father and children. Tenderness in fatherhood leads to the richest and strongest of all bonds— a lifetime love between a father and his children.

12 Tenderness in Brotherhood

The Primary Bond

Brotherhood is one of the strongest bonds men can know. Those of us who have been fortunate enough to know the intimate connection of this relationship are lucky indeed. It is a bond which not only survives contest and competition, but which often thrives on them. All of the fights and taunts of childhood are somehow transformed and matured into a deep bond that goes beyond language and is, truly, in the blood.

My own blood brother, Bob, is thirteen years younger than I am. We are the only two children in our family. For many years we were quite distant because of the differences in our ages. He seemed to me more like a son, and he was my pride and joy when he was born. I recall playing with him for hours on end. We would even fall asleep together on the floor when he was one and I was fourteen, exhausted from hours of crawling and child play together. My mother once took a photo of us both fallen asleep—me across his crib with him holding on to my nose with one of his little hands and holding my thumb with the other. I left home a few years later to "seek my fortune."

He was still an infant, and we grew apart for many years.

It is sad that my brother grew up with a superachiever image of his "great brother" to compete with. My father often held up an image of me as a model for my brother, an impossibly perfect model who (my father thought) did no wrong. Striving to be the overachiever I thought my father desired, I rarely shared my trials and mistakes and crises with him, but rather bore these burdens silently myself, depriving both of us of the joy of giving and receiving support. Thus, the only image my father knew of me was the "perfect" image—all achievements and no failures.

Though my brother is talented, I think he sensed that he could not compete with the model of me my father held for him, so he "dropped out." In some ways he is wiser than I, especially in the spiritual or mystical paths. In other ways he has suffered intense pain and loneliness—as I have—and our sharing of this has brought us closer.

Bob and I are only now beginning to explore our plans of being together in our adult years, sharing our lives more than we have in the past, and looking to each other for support and caring.

Recently, Bob wrote to send me his own thoughts about the place of tenderness in men's lives. Here is part of his letter:

Tenderness is a phenomenon, I believe, that comes from the conscious or subconscious awareness that there is, at root, a source common to both parties. People have in common their divinity and humanity, and possibly their sexuality, nationality and local affiliations.

There are times, though, when shared heritage at any level will be overshadowed by feelings of separateness and alienation. The most tender of lovers will occasionally become tough in defense of his individuality.

I have found that when I am not responsive to my wife it is usually because my ego feels threatened, as though to open up and be tender would be to lose myself. I think that it is important for a person to maintain his personhood and integrity but at the same time he must work toward recognizing the essence of himself in the rest of the world, and as he does this, he will become a more tender person.

Brotherhood provides a unique condition for the expression of tenderness. Brothers or sisters have more in common than people otherwise related. They have the same family and are equated more or less as peers in the family hierarchy.

Brotherhood, like marriage, can be an intimate, if not romantic coupling. It also shares a greater propensity for dislike or toughness, especially during the stage of sibling rivalry. But, if brothers or sisters can remain or become tender toward each other a really unique and wonderful relationship can develop.

A good family example to me of a healthy brotherhood is illustrated between the three brothers on the television show *Bonanza:* in spite of some macho-ness, they exemplify an expansive sense of fellowship and self-respect largely attributed to their brotherhood. They are not just three good friends, they are the *Cartwrights.* They share many of the same things: parents, environment, heritage, yet they are three distinct personalities. So, brotherhood can provide a kind of nest or soil for the cultivation of individuality, while providing also a broadened feeling of identity.

You and I have quite a poignant story as brothers. We never really have spent a lot of time together. The times that we have been together, though, have been memorable ones. One of the most memorable for me was a very tender expression of love and sympathy between us when our mother died. I was nine years old at the time and very deeply hurt. I remember you walking with me around the block of our house in Virginia sharing your sorrow with me and trying to help me understand the impossible. At that time, I wanted *nothing* more than a brother whom I could share my grief with. I had that with you.

I hope your book will do for some people what just the idea behind this chapter has done for me—that is, to bring to me an insight into a part of my life that I cherish, but will cherish now even more for becoming aware of it.

Love,
Bob

As Bob's letter makes clear, time and distance do not erase the primary bonds of brotherhood. This intimate blood tie provides many men fortunate enough to have blood brothers with an early and continuing "laboratory in tenderness."

Fraternal Brotherhood

There is also another kind of brotherhood which men can enjoy beyond the primary brotherhood of sharing the same mother and father. It is the fraternal feeling which men experience with one another. Just as women have discovered the strength and support of sisterhood, so men now are becoming more aware of the bonds of brotherhood. These bonds have existed for centuries. Soldiers in combat have known of the unusual camaraderie which only those who have been "in the arena" together can share. Those who compete in any arena know the particular feelings of closeness which can develop even between competitors.

One of the things I like most about brotherhood and the tenderness of men who are in this relationship is that it allows men to strive with one another, argue, contend, and compete —yet compete as brothers. It is a feeling based on mutual respect. Boxers who have battled each other for ten rounds often will fall into each other's arms and embrace when their match is over. They have come to know each other in a way that few people ever do. It is an intimacy born of pain and survival. Several professional athletes have told me that the sense of brotherhood they feel toward their toughest competitors is one that lasts their lifetimes.

I was discussing plans for an Olympics for gifted and talented youth of the world with Marty Glickman, a former Olympic sprinter. I suggested to him that we might emphasize non-competitive "no lose" games to de-emphasize competition in these Olympic games. He didn't agree. "Please don't take out the competition! The men that I am closest to in this world are those whom I ran against and who were my toughest competitors." General Douglas MacArthur said that "Upon the fields of friendly strife are sowed the seeds which upon other fields and in other days will bear the fruits of victory." Though the athletic field provides some macho conditioning which males need to move beyond in order to be whole, it also provides other unique opportunities for closeness.

In the same way, competitors in business often develop a strong feeling of affinity, even when they represent different companies or are competing for the same contract. They can see past the temporary limitations of the game they are playing to the essential humanity of the players. The name of the game doesn't matter. The important fact is that they participate together and share a bond. But even in a more ordinary way, men who are close friends and have built up a kind of history of friendship—their own brotherhood over time—can appreciate the bond they have that allows them to take risks together which they might not take with other people.

Camaraderie: Sharing Trials of Courage and Character

From my academy and military experience, one of the things that I found I missed most after leaving soldiering (there were many things I was delighted to leave behind) was the sense of brotherhood and camaraderie I had shared with my fellow Army officers who had survived the ordeals of West Point, paratrooper, or Ranger training together with me. This bond grew between those of us who had faced certain trials of courage and character together. We knew that we could count on one another when the chips were down, because we had been tested by these mutual survival experiences.

Some of the toughest Green Beret or Ranger Army officers can display tenderness very directly and openly. For example,

I recall from Ranger training that one of the most grueling patrols we had was a seventy-mile-long patrol in the dead of winter through the frozen mountains. Each of us had been assigned a "Ranger buddy." Ranger buddies came through for each other. You took care of your buddy and he took care of you. I can recall watching Rangers who weighed considerably more than their buddies being carried by their Ranger buddies and cared for like little children by them. I recall my own buddy's feet becoming frostbitten, and my trying to thaw them. We had eaten no food for twenty-four hours and were attempting to survive in sub-zero temperatures. He had fallen in a river, and his clothes had frozen. I took off his shoes and rubbed and massaged his feet and put them under my armpits to thaw them out. Other Rangers did similar things for their buddies. The bonds between us developed as we literally helped each other survive. We carried each other across the rivers. We carried our buddy's machine gun along with our own rifle when he was incapacitated. Such experiences build powerful bonds between men who have worked in survival situations together. And I have very much missed that sort of camaraderie—though not the survival trials themselves.

When I left the military, I went immediately into the academic world. There I found a kind of cutthroat competitiveness that was different from military competition. I naively found that people would "do you in" behind your back in "the outside world" in ways I hadn't experienced in the military. And I was very much nostalgic and hungry for the old camaraderie. This was a special kind of brotherhood and it was both characterized and strengthened by tenderness.

The Loneliness of the Hunter

Throughout history, men have created fraternal organizations to nurture the bond of brotherhood and to honor it. I think there *is* a special feeling between men which only men experience with one another—just as I am sure there is a whole range of emotions and responses which only women share together. These bonds are important for men, as they are for women. Like women, men face a special kind of loneliness in life: the loneliness of the hunter, the one who must seek his nourishment in a large and not always friendly world. Women seem to experience a different loneliness, the loneliness of the one who is taken for granted and left behind when the men leave on their hunt, whether this hunt takes them into the out back or to the office. Men seem to have to leave, and women to stay—at least this is the way the stereotype of male and female roles traditionally has been defined. Things may be changing now, yet I think there is a certain level at which these stereotypes are accurate. They exist in the literature of many cultures from ancient Greece to our own time. Penelope and Odysseus are the classic examples of what we now experience as the man commuting and the woman staying home. We may experience this distinction now in a degraded form, without the nobility of either Odysseus or Penelope, yet the loneliness of men and women remains.

To ease this loneliness, men tend to seek one another out, to give one another the kind of understanding and empathy which either women cannot give or which men have not learned to accept from women. The feeling which men have for one another can be very precious—and all the more so if these same men are not totally free in their emotional communication with women. I am sure this is why so many men enjoy going to their favorite bar to meet their buddies. It is not the drinking as much as the good feeling they can share which draws them there. In this all-male company, many men feel relaxed enough to let down their guard and emote freely with their brothers. Women may regard this as childish or crude, yet for many men

I am convinced it is a necessary outlet and release for the love which they may feel but not know how to communicate, even in their own families.

The Poet and the Soldier

I enjoy close relationships with "brothers" other than my blood brother. Friendship with a fraternal "brother" is a very special kind of love that men can share, one that men and women do not seem to share as readily.

It's deeper than the average friendship. It's the knowledge and the wisdom that you know you can count on that individual to support you, to care for you, to accept you, no matter how "bad" you may be. It is a basic acceptance of you as a human being. It grows from being men together, sharing the burdens of the sexual roles that you've both grown up in, and also the joys of those roles. Sometimes women don't understand this kind of love between men. For example, men who go hunting and fishing together often share this bond of brotherhood, one that can be tender even though it is between two males out on a hunting trip.

Whether with someone of the complementary or same sex, friendship is very much a form of love. The need to concentrate energy in a few love relationships, rather than diluting it in many, holds true for friendships as well. Friendship is love, and I am discovering that I do not sustain adequately more than three or four full-time friendships. I have many friends living all over the world, yet I do not classify most of them as full-time "brothers." The full-time ones are those I draw nourishment from and provide nourishment to on a day-to-day basis.

Such friends, or "brothers," are precious people who like you just the way you are. They have no personal improvement program for you. It is important to look for these few relationships that really lift and sustain you. These are the ones to begin devoting more of your energy and time to. I find I miss how much their nurturing really means to me when I dilute these special ones with all the many average relationships and contacts I have. And when I do this I miss much out of life. It is like diluting paint down with thinner. It will cover more of the house, but it won't hold up as long. Such "brothers" are people who check in with me from time to time just to make sure everything is going well. This is important to me, because when I am troubled I am least likely to call on someone for help. As I become older I realize how important these few people are, and how much it means for them to come to me often, just as I go to them often. This is a recent realization for me, because I tended to take the old friends for granted. The interesting thing is that friends who like me just the way I am assist me to grow. As I spend more of my time with them, they provide a space for me to become more of whatever I am capable of being.

I am rich in having one or two of these deep brothers whom I can count on when trouble and problems arise, whom I can trust to provide an honest reaction rather than a tactful or polite one. A brother is one who accepts me, not for what I *have done*, but because *I am*—good and bad, strong and weak.

One of my closest friends and "brothers" is Gabriel Heilig, who is collaborating with me in the preparation of much of the material for this book. Our friendship began at a time when we were both vulnerable. We had both just separated from our wives and were beginning the crises of exploring our loneliness after some years of marriage.

Gabriel's background was vastly different from mine. While I had been surviving the discipline of the military and the bureaucracy, Gabriel had been attending Antioch College, a free and creative environment. He explored literature and creative writing and became a poet, while I was exploring engineering, military leadership, and academic administration—just the opposite of creativity in some ways. During my military years Gabe was a conscientious objector. Again the paradox of polarities attracting—the poet and the soldier.

When we met, I was just beginning to open myself to the exciting realms of my human and creative potential. Gabriel shared music, poems, novels, and ideas with me. He had a strong desire to use his considerable creativity to make the world a more human and effective place through education and government. I shared my knowledge, contacts, and experience of the bureaucracy and political power with him. We both shared our pain, our loneliness, and some beautiful adventures together. We both grew and profited from that beginning of brotherhood together.

Our love as "brothers" has grown steadily over the years. Gabriel has helped me to experience, perhaps more than any other brother or friend, my own tenderness as a man. I had never really allowed another man to openly share so much tenderness with me before. I had always masked or camouflaged it in the ways that tenderness often masquerades itself—military camaraderie, athletic fellowship, or the macho affection of hunting and fishing buddies—all genuine expressions of tenderness but not as direct and open and vulnerable as my friendship with Gabriel. There was nothing of a homosexual nature about this expression of love between us, yet it was entirely free of the rigid sex roles that had been conditioned in us. Still, I'm sure that I would have worried five years earlier about "how we looked" to others, we were so close. And this fear on my part would have gotten in the way of my having the great gift of the brotherhood that I'd shared with Gabriel.

I will share the poem Gabe wrote for my birthday:

MOON BROTHERS*

for Hal Lyon

I write this one for you,
my brother,

strong, and loose, and
clear as the wilderness midnight's
mountain cat,
that sits and waits
to leap across the goddess moon.
We each must dare
to find our loves,
our fates.

How to weave the time we share
this way in words?
How to fix in images
the power that is there,
or feel my love flow through
these reaching arms of rhyme,
and thin reason's measure?

Reason stops somewhere,
and the night begins.

Our lives and seasons—
what are they but
the star-shine shimmer
on the black cat's back?

We are strong, brother.
We will wait,
patient as the cat waits
for the night's first lady
to appear—

to cross in the eye,
and then to leap,
and the arrow of the heart
to fly.

For us,
the full moon
is our mother.
The bond we share
is old as stone.

I light a candle,
say a prayer:

May the cat's eye
guard and guide you,
brother,
light your brow,
and lead you home.

13 Tenderness in Public and Professional Life

> After you understand all about the sun and
> the stars and the rotation of the earth, you may
> still miss the radiance of the sunset.
> ALFRED NORTH WHITEHEAD

It may be difficult to see how tenderness can have any place whatsoever in public or professional life. For many of us our professional lives are personal wars in which we feel we must either win or lose, stand or fall. Rather than make a contribution through our careers, often we try to prove our worth, our ability, our manhood. Perceived this way, tenderness seems a luxury or even an illusion in professional life.

Yet I have repeatedly found that tenderness has been invaluable to me in my work as a professional person. Even in the Army I found that a humanistic approach in leadership was extremely useful in producing positive results. And in business, as in the Army, results count.

A Non-Bureaucracy Within the Bureaucracy

Several years ago I began to be more openly tender, not only with my friends, but also at my work in the government. I was rewarded by some of my friends, and I felt myself accepting them for themselves and feeling closer to them as I did it. I then resolved to try this within the bureaucracy.

I had been asked to help organize a new bureau in my department. The first day in the life of the bureau, I assembled all the people and told them that I felt we were small enough and new enough to create an experimental non-bureaucratic organization within the bureaucracy, if they were willing to participate. I suggested that we might even build an organization which would be enjoyable for all of us to work in.

We broke down into twelve-person leaderless groups, and set aside our work commitments to explore such issues as "What gives us the most pain in our working environment?" and "How can we get rid of the most undesirable aspects of bureaucratic work?" I also shared with them the research of Rensis Likert on high- and low-producing managers. Some time before, Dr. Likert had gone into 5000 organizations of various types and identified the high-producing managers and the low producers, eliminating from his study all the average or questionable producers. The results were fascinating to me.

The high producers were very "people-oriented." People were unique individuals to them. Low producers, on the other hand, were "production-oriented." To them, people were tools to get the job done.

The high producers were good delegators; the low producers were not. The high producers allowed their subordinates to participate in decisions; the low producers were very autocratic. The high producers were relatively non-punitive; the low producers were quite punitive. The high producers had a good open two-way personal communication flow; the low producers were closed and relatively inaccessible.

The high producers had few formal meetings, at which only one or two people spoke. They didn't have to meet often, since

they had such open communication flow. This is especially interesting, judging by the frequency of meetings in the bureaucracy. The low producers, on the other hand, had frequent and
quite formal meetings at which only the chiefs spoke, usually to
give explicit instructions.

The high producers had a lot of pride in their work groups.
The low producers were surrounded by low morale. The high
producers planned ahead effectively. They weren't just soft or
goody-goody human-relations types. The low producers didn't
plan well. They gave orders to people, but they didn't plan with
them.

In times of crisis the high producers maintained their super-
visory roles, whereas the low producers would get immediately
involved with details. So when another crisis developed, there
was no supervisor to send to the crisis area.*

I suggested to my bureau people that perhaps we could look
at ourselves in terms of these traits to see if we might move
toward the people-oriented, high-producer style of management. I explained that few managers have all the high-producer
traits, but they make the most of those they have. Likert's
research showed that there are situations—crisis deadline situations—in which the low producer style is more effective. (I
should have known that from my earlier work in government,
since there the "crisis-management" approach is the order of
the day!)

I had previously experimented with these traits of the high
and the low producer four years earlier when serving in a top-
echelon government job. In a memo to the agency head, I
presented these traits and suggested that after six months of
serving in the organization I saw the traits of the low producer

*Rensis Likert, *New Patterns of Management* (New York: McGraw-Hill,
1961).

every day, everywhere I looked. Apparently the office had grown so dynamically in the mid-1960s with the passage of massive new federal legislation that many production-oriented individuals were brought in to get the crisis job done. I even went so far in my memo as to scramble all the high- and low-producer traits in a checklist, with the suggestion that my boss (followed by each bureau chief) have his subordinates rate him on a checklist, not telling them what it was about until afterward, then revealing that they had just rated him on high- and low-producer traits and how he had scored. I felt that the bureau chiefs, by using this as a vehicle for open leadership discussions with their division directors, might have some good results. I suggested that then the division directors could do the same thing with their branch chiefs.

I was naive. The boss sent my leadership memo to the bureau chiefs. I was overwhelmed by the defensive reactions! One chief fired off a memo that I was new and thus just didn't understand that the office had grown so dynamically in program but so little in personnel that there wasn't time to do the work, much less time for such "self-improvement" exercises.

However, one brave bureau chief decided to try the experiment. He felt good about the experience initially; but his bureau, the largest in the office, had the most problems and the most entrenched division directors. He left government service several months later.

My boss approved my recommendation to make one last-ditch try with the top ten leaders in the office by bringing in Chris Argyris, noted author of management books and a professor at Yale. We instituted quarterly retreats where top managers from the office gathered at a remote setting, and we asked Chris to act as a facilitator. He began trying to slice through the complex network of hidden agendas that were surfacing at our policy meetings. Several people were both shocked and offended as he accurately revealed what was really going on behind the saccharine words of one of our distinguished bureau chiefs.

For a while I was heartened at the new level of honesty that began to appear. I even hoped that our bureau chiefs were going to begin working cooperatively like a board of governors for the office, sharing resources to develop jointly funded projects. In fact, we did. One was the North Dakota humanistic-education project, in which we packaged eleven different federal legislative authorities together to improve education at every level in that state. However, as chairman of the task force which pulled that plan together, I must admit that when the people-oriented management style failed among my bureaucratic colleagues, I resorted to more autocratic means to force the various program officers to bend their policies to fit the needs of this exciting project.

At about that time, we experienced a change of administrations, with President Nixon replacing President Johnson. As the search for new political appointees dragged on, a long year of stagnation plagued our office. Fortunately for me, I was off to a stimulating year of growth at the University of Massachusetts. But the retreats soon disappeared, or rather changed into "planning sessions," with little attention paid to group dynamics or the human process that was at the heart of them—or should have been.

So after all these earlier efforts, here I was again at a new bureau attempting to create a non-bureaucratic organization within the bureaucracy, flying in the face of all the principles of bureaucracies advanced by Max Weber and the other authorities on organizations who say that bureaucracies need to be impersonal and have red tape in order to protect the public trust and to prevent individuals from taking advantage of them.

After sharing my views on people-oriented management and breaking bureau personnel down into small groups, I went around and spent time with each group. I was heartened by some of the things I saw taking place. In one group a secretary was saying, "Well, what I'd like to see in our new bureau is equality. I know my boss outranks me in the civil service system, and I accept that, but he doesn't outrank me as a human being! Every day when he walks into the office, he lets me know, without even speaking, that I am a non-professional and he is a professional. I'd like to write him a list of the ten things that would make me appreciate my boss more!" Her boss, who was in the room, snapped back, "Well, why don't you do it!" She replied, "I will if you won't get me fired." (Hardly anyone can get fired in the federal civil service unless he is a political appointee.) Her boss rejoined, "I'd like to make you a list of the ten things that would make me appreciate my secretary more!" With a tear running down her face, she softly replied, "If you did that, it would be the first time in four years that you have said anything good *or* bad about how I've worked for you." He stepped over and hugged her stiffly (but it was a hug!). They both started laughing and began talking, for the first time in four years, as equal human beings!

This kind of successful experience fanned the flame of my desire to do more. Though the experiment seemed to be working among the lower-ranking employees, few upper-echelon managers responded well. In fact, the most common response was a defensive entrenching and tightening up. Many of the top staff felt threatened as their junior people began to coordinate and communicate freely and laterally with other organizations and vertically with people above their own bosses.

It was then that I realized what should have been apparent to me long before: that bureaucracies often attract the kind of people who *value* the security of a hierarchical chain of command. Many of these individuals want everything to flow through them. Basically, they don't trust others to operate on their own. So my experiment in trying to make a non-bureaucratic organization within the bureaucracy, though not exactly a failure, was not really a success either.

Finally, after two years of working to build the new non-bureaucratic bureau, the opportunity was offered me to continue my work in humanistic education by trying to get a national effort going on behalf of one of the country's most seriously neglected minority groups—gifted children. My hunch was that humanistic education was one of the principal ways to reach these youngsters, many of whom have the potential to make major social and artistic contributions to our world. Part of my feeling came from some earlier work I had done in 1968 as a consultant to a White House task force on the gifted.

At that time the task force went around the country interviewing some of the country's most successful men and women. The question was put to them: "What single factor could you identify, if any, which helped you most to realize your potential?" I was amazed that almost every one of them had the identical response. In each of their lives, someone—a teacher, a coach, or some other respected person—had dropped his roles and masks, his rank and status, and built an intimate one-to-one human relationship with them, encouraging them to believe in themselves as human beings and encouraging them to step out and take far more risks than they would have done without such encouragement. Once again Fritz Perls and his stretching of ego boundaries, Carl Rogers and his "prizing" of another individual's uniqueness! For all of us, this is the kind of support that leads us to discover ourselves and realize our potential. Such opportunities for one-to-one human relationships without the usual masks and roles had been altogether too rare in most of my own formal education.

In my work directing the federal effort for gifted and talented youth—potentially the future leaders of the world—I once again saw the need for a tender, humanistic approach. If we do anything for the gifted and talented—and fewer than 4 percent of them are being adequately served—we tend to push them down the purely cognitive or intellectual track, with little attention at all paid to their feelings and affective development. Often considerable hostility is directed toward these youngsters by their peers and their teachers. These children are the ones who ask the threatening and penetrating questions in class. Also, a false notion prevails that they will make it on their own, when in fact the dropout ranks are filled with gifted and talented youth who were turned off by the traditional lockstep classroom. I felt and openly advocated from a national forum that along with their intellectual development, we should nourish their capacities for love, empathy, and awareness. Without those traits, their other gifts would be wasted.

I also pushed for a creative national approach to this neglected minority group of American children. I went hat in hand to private foundations and donors seeking the financial support the federal government did not have the legislation to provide. Working with Educational Expeditions International and the Explorer's Club, we established a national Exploration Scholarship Program which became so successful that over 6000 gifted youngsters applied for scholarships to accompany some of the world's leading scientists on global expeditions as working members of scientific teams. Some went to Greece, where they spent three hours a day surveying the ancient city of Sparta. Others went to the Congo to study the molten lava lakes with one of the world's greatest volcanologists. A gifted youngster from Harlem who had built his own telescope at age twelve and who was tutoring other youths on his rooftop was selected to accompany scientists to the Sahara Desert to study the total eclipse of the sun.

These one-to-one human mentorships literally transformed

the lives of many of these youngsters. Yet, I had exceeded the bureaucracy's willingness to be bold, imaginative, and creative. Every success was met with growing criticism and resistance from within the bureaucracy—but with considerable applause from the field, where new national leadership was greeted with enthusiasm. For the first few years we were able to accomplish a great deal, before the red tape and resistance began to have its effect on us. This was partially because we did so much so boldly and so quickly with few federal resources. We finally succeeded in getting national legislation passed through the Congress, thanks in particular to Senator Jacob Javits, our prime supporter.

And then the red tape really began to limit our creative endeavors—paradoxically, a sign of progress in the bureaucracy. However, a humanistic approach prevailed in the national philosophy, and it was gratifying to see so many in the field beginning to consider integrating emotional concerns for gifted youth into their intellectual programs.

For a variety of reasons, I left on a two-year detail to an academic-community setting to develop a non-athletic "Olympics" of the mind and senses for gifted youth of the world.

I have mixed feelings about those five years. At times the least appropriate behavior for survival within the bureaucracy or industry is tenderness. There were times when I needed all my toughness, and then some. Toughness *is* appropriate when you are being shot at. Tenderness is foolishness at those times. But we cannot live all our lives in trenches. Emotional trenches quickly become emotional graves.

Humanistic Management and Awareness

I remember a saying of a former boss, Vernon Alden, who as president of Ohio University ushered me through the troublesome transition from a totally military life to a civilian life. He used to say that if a major-league baseball player decided to lead the league in batting by trying to bat .400 he would never even make the team. But rather he must try to hit 1000—that is, to try to get a hit every time at bat. And then, if he is indeed great, he might end up hitting .350 or .400.

This meshes well with my own views of goal-oriented behavior. I feel that if you have had good, substantial tastes of success early in your life, success can become a way of life for you and you can refuse to settle for less.

Unconsciously you will then automatically crank in feedback, keeping yourself on the trail to success, whatever it is you are pursuing. As we progress through life, there are many side trails leading to failure and many obstacles along the way. The success-oriented person automatically increases his energy and gets over the obstacles, often homing in on a goal of succeeding, refusing to settle for less. The pessimistic person takes the first trail leading to failure and fails (which is the goal to which *he* is oriented), then he says, "I failed. I knew I would."

The bind I get into about this is my past tendency to try to be perfect, to think I could accomplish whatever I willed. Perhaps this is largely true—one can accomplish almost anything if he is willing to pay the price. Often, however, the price may be my aliveness, my feelings. I am no longer willing to pay that price.

I recall being in a session fighting for my office's budget. The budget process is such a demeaning one, with your estimates gradually and painfully amputated to a fraction of what you initially requested, that it is common practice to oversell and exaggerate. I recall at this meeting experiencing an awful feeling in my stomach as I was overselling. Then I thought to myself, I'm glad I feel bad. As long as I feel bad when I oversell, I am still aware of the price I pay playing big-league bureaucracy games. When I no longer feel bad when I'm lying, then I will be in trouble. I will have taken on these games as a way of life, really believing the roles I'm playing—like so many bureaucrats who take it all seriously and believe their own role playing. I don't want to lose my awareness.

The Tender Politician

Is it possible that in a profession as thick-skinned as the world of politics a tender individual can succeed? Observers of Senators Muskie, McGovern, and Eagleton would more than likely join the ranks of those who would answer this question with a resounding *no!* But these strong men, who have exhibited such politically dangerous behavior as crying, or being openly honest, or having been in therapy, still do survive. In fact, they succeed. The question is What price do we agree to pay for success? These men are successful even though they lost some fights—for reasons of integrity, I would add.

Such men are tender *and* strong, and I feel their strength and success are greater because of their willingness to be tender. They are not willing to have "success" as politics defines it, at any price. And now a whole new breed of young politicians is being voted to Washington by people who respect them for their integrity.

The recent violations of public trust—in Vietnam, in Watergate, in the abuses of police powers by the FBI and the CIA—indicate that the hard-nosed patriot often leaves out a lot of reality in the world picture that he sees. The world is not a simple landscape etched in black and white. It is more like a kaleidoscope in which shapes keep changing. In such a world, vigilance is surely required. There is no point in being naive. But vigilantism is something else again. Dividing the world up into "us" and "them" virtually guarantees a shrinking world—for any person or group that thinks this way. The experience of

the Nixon Presidency is a sad and sobe
truth. Eventually the poison of distrust s
system and infects everyone. Everyo
Trust is destroyed. The basis for dece
There is no longer government then

The recent election of Jimmy Carter ᴵᴄ,
by the American people that a climate of basic ᴵᴵᵁ_
needs to be restored to our public life. It is not enough to ᵇᵉ
tough to our adversaries. We must also be decent and tender
with one another—otherwise, what is the point of creating a
society? Our country is called the *United* States of America.
What keeps us unified is our trust and our willingness to be
tender toward one another—to challenge others to do their
best, yes, but not to create such deep divisions that we work
against one another out of continuing spite.

It has taken over a hundred years for the wounds of the Civil
War to heal and for a Southerner to be elected President. His
election was not a fluke. It was a sign that some things count
more than the artificial toughness which men like Nixon displayed. Sincerity, compassion, and tenderness have a place
ahead of brute strength in creating America as the nation we
want it to be.

Jimmy Carter showed perhaps his greatest strength in that
tender and human moment when he returned to his home
town of Plains, Georgia, let his political roles and masks fall
away, and cried. He had the strength to allow his feelings to
surface in their own way rather than to interrupt their flow. As
that scene was captured by the television camera, millions of
Americans all over the country, even many of those who did not
vote for him, gained the realization that a real human being—
vulnerable, tender, and also strong—had been elected to the
Presidency. Carter's spiritual and moral strength may be able
to fill a vacuum which has existed in the Presidency for some

This feeling may be in large part why a majority of the
American voters elected him to office. President Carter can
serve America well by continuing to communicate as a man
with real feelings, rather than a programmed "Presidential"
robot. We need more true feeling in our public life, not less.

A friend of mine, John Vasconcellos, is one of the most tender politicians I have ever known personally. He lives a humanistic life style, not just as a political image, but in his everyday
life, and he works this way with his staff, his colleagues, and his
constituents. He has been repeatedly reelected to the California Legislature, where he serves as Chairman of the powerful
Higher Education Subcommittee. In the brief statement that
follows he shares some of his own reflections on tenderness in
his public life as a politician.

These past eleven years I've gone through incredible—and enlightening—changes. I campaigned as a very straight, stiff traditional
crew-cut intellectual liberal. Today I am remarkably and noticeably
looser, with medium-long hair (having miraculously survived my long-
hair period), a tradition-challenging earthy radical in the proper sense
of that term: "Committed to going to the very root of political problems."

Initially I had little sense of the relatedness of my personal and
political lives. A year with a Carl Rogers-trained priest-psychologist
enabled me to survive the crucial state of my identity crisis, shored up
by Sidney Jourard's *The Transparent Self.* In 1969 I spent about one
weekend a month in some form of growth experience with friends,
exploring whether and how the human potential movement and politics connect—and if so, how we could go about converging them. Then
I took up bioenergetics, a modernization of Reichian theory which
seeks to liberate the connections between the body and emotions and
intellect of the entire person. From then on I have been seeing ever
more clearly the connections between becoming a person and being
a relevant and effective politician in our society.

The politics we do is who we are! For how I experience myself as a person provides me the vision I carry into all my relationships—interpersonal and institutional.

I have come to recognize that what is commonly perceived to be the breakdown of our society is in reality a break*through*. Bill Harmon of Stanford Research Institute has characterized our times as "The New Copernican Revolution," succeeding the revolutions of Copernicus and Galileo, of Darwin and of Freud. Today we are going through perhaps the ultimate phase of liberation struggle: that is to free ourselves from psychological bondage. No one wants to be owned by anyone else. Many of us are reaching for and searching out how much more we can become, express, and share ourselves in ways that are mutually enhancing rather than the destructive ways that institutions have used to deal with people in this country and elsewhere for a long time.

What has this to do with "tenderness"? Insofar as this personal political revolution is precisely about what it means to be human, tenderness is a major part of the issue. My sense is that tenderness is natural to humanness and critical for fulfilling life itself. Tenderness ought not to be seen as a means to an end (strength). Rightly, tenderness is the natural expression of the only true end—to become fully human.

Humanistic Education

In education also a tender and humanistic approach is crucial. For many years I have been a professional educator practicing what I would call a humanistic approach, encouraging teachers to take off their masks and look at students as persons instead of playing the teacher role. Giving up roles has application to our relationships in all walks of life, and school is as good a place as any to learn this.

I'm not advocating that we become amateur therapists in the classroom or elsewhere—teachers are not legally or professionally qualified to do that—but I am saying that we should be human in the classroom. When this happens, we begin to allow people to *be*.

It's not so easy to take such a simple risk. To stand up in front of a class and recognize that you're not a superior being lecturing down at an inferior group of students whom you're going to fill up with your great knowledge can be very frightening—and also very freeing. This is the difference between what I call "status" and "natural" authority. The status-authority teacher who insists on lecturing down *at* a collective group of students is hiding behind his or her title, degrees, and podium. This teacher is not relevant to the students in most classrooms today. Our children want authenticity, not autocracy.

The relevant teacher is one who has natural authority—earned from sharing in a learning experience with people who are equals as human beings. This is the teacher who can share fully, bringing to bear all of his or her resources: books, experiences, friends, and the other students in the classroom who know something special. The "learning facilitator" who can bring a student out communicates this natural authority.

As teachers, or in other professions (in life, for that matter), we don't have to have all the answers. For me this was a tremendous discovery! When I realized that I no longer had to be perfect, despite the fact that some of society's institutions rewarded me for pretending to be, a tremendous burden was lifted from my shoulders.

We have many one-dimensional "half-men" teaching all around the country, people often brilliantly developed intellectually but stunted emotionally. Many of them are afraid to deal with their feelings, and instead try to ignore their own emotions —and their students. These are the teachers who rely on their status authority, lecturing in a purely cognitive way that emphasizes only the intellectual and is void of affect or feeling. But life, even in the classroom, is more than just a set of notes.

This is not the kind of "learning facilitator" Carl Rogers thinks a teacher should be. One dictionary definition of "teach" is "to make to know how." Who wants to *make* someone know something? Rogers wants to allow students to *discover* things, and to encourage them in these discoveries. The kinds of learning experiences which last are those of discovery. I like the term "discovery facilitator" even better.

Abraham Maslow suggested that the peak experiences in life—even the tragedies and crises—are things that we should treasure. These are the times in life when deep learning takes place. They are largely emotional, but also cognitive. Maslow says:

We must learn to treasure the jags of the child in the school, his fascination, absorptions, his persistent wide-eyed wondering, his Dionysian enthusiasm . . . They can lead to much. Especially they can lead to hard work, persistence, absorbed fruitful education.*

These are things that we should learn to foster in the classroom instead of denying the emotions of children. Emotions are energy. We should use this energy, not ignore it.

When we realize we no longer have to have all the answers, we can begin being real, imperfect human beings. The thing that's beautiful about people is not a put-on "perfection," which many teachers try to achieve. Those people who are overly protected—who have tried to be "perfect," who have the narrow ego boundaries that society draws for us—are also not so colorful. They don't have the flavor of people who are more natural. Who wants a perfect teacher? What's beautiful is our humanity, which means we are real and imperfect.

I'm convinced that if we can deal with the whole person in the classroom, if teachers can begin to deal with children as

*Abraham H. Maslow, "Some Education Implications of the Humanistic Psychologies," *Harvard Educational Review* 38, No. 4 (Fall 1968): p. 689

feeling human beings instead of just intellects to be developed, then there is enormous hope for education. I define humanistic education as cognitive—intellectual—learning *plus* affective learning. We *can* integrate the two; and when we do, both peak.

There are different camps in the humanistic-education movement. There are groups which want to develop a purely affective curriculum—one that could be delivered like physical education in a separate block of instruction. There are other groups which want to integrate the cognitive with the affective within the classroom. Both approaches hold merit. What we cannot afford to do is nothing.

I mentioned earlier the traits that Carl Rogers thinks really count in therapy. He and his colleagues are beginning to find empirical evidence that these traits are also present in the effective teacher. They rest on four things: realness in the facilitator, a sense of prizing another individual, a sense of trust, and a sense of empathy. Now, these are traits very few schools of education are teaching. It's hard to teach them. You have to let people discover them. Yet you also have to provide an environment in which such discoveries can take place. I feel these are the very traits that also work in business, in all types of professional relationships, and in interpersonal relationships with those whom we care about most. Moreover, they are the traits that enable us to take the step from environmental to self-support—to love ourselves and to reach that conscious, "centered" place where we are free from being slaves to everyone else's desires or "shoulds."

When this happens and we reach that place, we reach another release, for which I have no explanation (and I'm not going to look for any, as I'm sure the phenomenon would disappear as soon as I intellectualized it). We become a mirror for the world and the people around us. We become clear.

When other people look into our eyes, they can feel their own beauty in the reflection then. It is as though we show them themselves, and they feel good about themselves. There is no intellectual explanation for that. It's just something that happens. My fantasy is that teachers can free themselves enough to become mirrors for their students in which the students can see the beauty of themselves as human beings, or that managers do the same with their employees. Then we would have truly humanistic education and management. We have a long way to go, and—slowly—I think we are getting there.

Humanistic Psychology

In my work as a psychologist and therapist, I also find a softer approach to be effective. There are many precedents for tenderness in the practice of psychology. Dr. Carl Rogers stands as the prime example. There is even an entire professional association for therapists with a more tender approach. This is the Association for Humanistic Psychology. Humanistic psychology, though it embraces the work of all other fields of psychology, is concerned primarily with the total evolution of the individual human being. In truth, none of us fit the sociological "averages." In our pain and our joys, the unique experiences which make us all different, we all defy the "averages" we're supposed to fit into.

But even among this group of supposedly humanistic professionals, tenderness is often masked. I can recall a personal experience at an annual convention of this association. I was leading a session. Prior to beginning, I found myself feeling threatened by the beards, robes, and sandals sitting around me dropping names with all the latest hip jargon: "When Alan Watts, another dude, and I were camped out in the high Sierras, we . . ."

Though I had been active in the human potential movement for some years and always enjoyed stretching my ego boundaries at these conventions, I generally found myself to be more of a link between the establishment (which many of the humanistic psychologists had written off) and the human potential movement. And I felt somewhat apart from my more hip colleagues.

When I led my own group at the convention, I risked opening to them the fearful feelings I felt at being confronted with such a group of "guru" therapists. I also shared how lonely that made me feel, and how much loneliness I saw among some of the people wearing their "together" masks at the convention. Openness and radicalness actually became defenses for some people at these meetings. You can hide quite effectively behind a statement of being a "radical."

But being a radical involves more than being loud (in dress or in speech), and more than the latest rhetoric. It also requires being *real*. The word "radical" comes from the Latin word meaning "root." A true radical is someone who goes to the root of things.

I found as I opened myself to this audience that some of the people I feared most responded that they, too, were lonely. I experienced a growing closeness with this group as we talked and shared. With the tenderness came a flow of strength, rather than the weakness that often had been covered up by my well-practiced speeches. I found that I suddenly felt closer to the "gurus" with whom I had felt so uncomfortable before, and that the fear that had kept us apart melted as we began to share our tender feelings instead of acting tough and falsely "together" with one another.

Transformations at the Organizational Level

It is one major accomplishment for us to liberate ourselves as tender men in our own personal lives. Yet it is quite another thing to carry this over into our professional careers. Such breakthroughs are better called transformations than changes. A transformation is essentially different from a change. We all make minor adjustments in our lives from time to time. These are changes, rather than transformations. A transformation is such a completely new way of being that it represents, and is, a basic shift in our whole experience and perspective.

The man who has transformed himself from being tough to being tender will find his experience of life to be completely different. I can "change" my pen by smashing it. It will be changed in form, but still the same material. If I turn it into something completely different, such as gold, I have transformed it completely.

In George Leonard's book *The Transformation* he writes of the current period in our history—a period of rapid change, and a time when many people are beginning to explore the inner frontiers of human consciousness. He considers this to be a time for our evolution through transformations. He even suggests plans for a new Transformation candidate who would be concerned with personal and organizational transformations.

Werner Erhard, the architect and founder of est (Latin for "it is"), the transformation training which has attracted over 100,000 Americans, claims that est is not about helping people change. That occurs from effort. Such changes are limited. Erhard wants to provide people an opportunity to experience *transformation* in their lives. Transformation involves the embracing of the inner self, which is already complete and perfect, and then remanifesting this experience of one's own self in one's personal daily universe.

The risks and rewards of "transformation" are well expressed in a recent letter jointly signed by John Denver, the folk singer; Robert Fuller, past President of Oberlin College and now Executive Director of the est Foundation; and Werner Erhard. I quote from it in some detail:

It is our observation that generally it is not safe for people to admit that their lives are transformed. Any indication that one's life is transformed is likely to provoke disbelief, if not scorn. There are at least two sources for this. First, there is the fear that others will think we have been conned. And, second, there is the feeling that others will interpret such an assertion to mean that we are saying that the events of our life are exclusively wonderful. In other words, "transformation" is widely misunderstood to signify that one who has experienced it knows nothing but joy and bliss. That is not what we mean. . . .

To say that one's life is transformed means that one has gotten off the position that one's life does *not* work. We have noticed that we are, each of us, willing to get off the position that our lives do not work, that things are "bad" or "wrong."

Our lives do work. That is to say, what is so in our lives is so. Our lives are the contexts of the events of our living, whatever those events may be. In this way, our lives are complete, whole and thereby satisfying.

We know that this is also true for you, and you are also committed to making it less risky for other people to experience and acknowledge transformation. Acknowledging to ourselves and to you that we are all members of this "conspiracy" to make the world a safer place for personal and social transformation brings us clarity of purpose and a sense of relatedness as we go about our business. In fact, the original meaning of "conspiracy" is to "breathe together," which expresses exactly what we have in mind. *We are together.* We are sharing our experience of alignment with you because the experience is enabling, freeing and supportive. We'd like to extend the "conspiracy" to you. . . .

As has been suggested in earlier chapters, there are many ways for personal transformation to occur. A personal transformation can happen to individuals through many forms of therapeutic growth. More frequently, what occurs is the temporary and incremental process of change rather than the complete miracle of transformation. Much of this book has dealt with the process of personal transformation from a tough way of being to a totally new and tender way of being. Change or transformation? Make your own exploration, and see.

So transformation can occur at the level of the individual, at the level of the individual in relationships with others and at the level of the individual in organizations. The most important and primary work is that to be done personally at the level of the individual, and in relationship with others.

Once you have really owned your own tenderness and the strength it provides you, and once you have learned to share it with others, how can you transform yourself at the levels of the organizations you find yourself in as you go about pursuing your career? The tender individual is quite vulnerable in the average organization. His tenderness can be killed off all too easily in the harsh and competitive battleground. Even those organizations which on the surface seem to be gentler than most can be quite deadly in subtle but equally lethal ways.

It is vital for the tender individual to link up with other tender people in mutual support groups. The support of others in any minority group—and tender males are definitely a minority—is crucial for the survival of the minority group's cause as well as its individual members.

A personal experience may help to illustrate this point better than a theoretical account. I spent several years, as I've mentioned, in a personal quest within the federal bureaucracy to grant more attention and support to a humanistic approach to both education and management. I realized that as an advocate of "humanistic education" I was a member of a minority group. I had written a textbook, which looked at the humanistic education movement and openly identified me as a proponent. I had also chaired the task force which founded the humanistic North Dakota project that Charles Silberman described in his book *Crisis in the Classroom.*

In taking a controversial position one is bound to run into criticism. Though I no longer feel it necessary to satisfy or be accepted by everyone, neither do I necessarily have to wage war against those who differ with my views. There will always be critics or enemies as long as one is making progress. A sure sign of progress, innovation, or successful pioneering is the clamor of those who will appear on the scene to resist any change in the old order. In an ultra-right-wing magazine an article bitterly attacked me and the views expressed in my textbook. The article contained many misquotes and wrong inferences and attempted to create the impression that because I was for "humanizing" education I proposed manipulating and "homogenizing" America's children.

The piece was widely (and effectively) distributed. It precipitated many letters to Washington asking that I be investigated. My bosses received letters from key Senators and Congressmen asking for an investigation of me, to which I had to submit at the cost of several weeks of my time, time that could have been better used in efforts to benefit children.

There were several lessons in this for me. One was that I should not try to sell my views on humanistic education as "innovations." After all, the best teachers have been treating their students in a human way for years. I also discovered as I listened and learned from several of my humanistic-education colleagues—Mike Arons, John Vasconcellos, Bill Bridges, and Bill Allen (all of whom have made strong humanistic inroads in conservative areas)—that conservatives hold strongly to their own cornerstones of security: concepts like honesty, responsibility, and even love—all of which, coincidentally, are also the cornerstones of humanistic education. Perhaps there was no need for me to knock heads with these conservatives, when I was really preaching honesty, responsibility, and love—the same things that they value. An important lesson for me! Besides, to put too much energy into the impossible task of being accepted by everyone was not taking care of myself or my energy. I must have been standing for some good things to have received such attention.

I experienced being very much alone in many of these struggles. There was a large body of humanistic educators, also alone out in the country, many of whom applauded my efforts, yet I was a loner on the firing line of the federal bureaucracy.

When a loyal friend who has been called a "militant humanist," Dave Aspy, joined me to help me fight for the programs I believed in, it is difficult to describe how much it meant to me to have even one person I knew who was totally on my side. It was as though ten strong persons had joined me, not just one. My friend Sam Halperin also joined with me in a somewhat quieter but also effective way to bring a more humanistic approach to education and government. We began conspiring ("breathing together") to expose top policymakers in Washington to humanistic thinkers like Carl Rogers, George Leonard, Moshe Feldenkrais, Bernie Gunther, and others through the forum of seminars for policymakers to which these outstanding humanists were invited.

It is so easy for the majority opposition to kill off the loner, no matter how strong he may be. Humanistic teachers, managers, and psychologists who take the lonely trek by themselves in hostile environments are often crushed as soon as they begin to effect changes in the status quo. Their very success dooms them. Those who have survived best usually have developed mutual support networks with other concerned individuals.

Good ideas can travel fast—if one is willing to communicate them. "Heroes" who fight alone also die alone. Allies who are willing to get as well as give support last a lot longer.

A Path with Heart: Tenderness Between Nations

Philip Noel-Baker, 1959 winner of the Nobel Peace Prize, stated during the 1976 Disarmament Forum in England that the most important single task any statesman could perform today would be to lead the world to comprehensive disarmament. In our world, where millions are malnourished and our environment is threatened increasingly, it is tragic and colossally foolish that our national 1978 fiscal budget includes a military appropriation of $114 billion—while our budget for education is less than 10 percent of that figure. Collectively, the nations of the world spend over $300 billion annually in an arms race which assures neither security nor peace. It is high time for us to see that we can build a world community far more effectively by making peace than by threatening war. We must use our resources, not use them up. We must defeat hunger, disease, and poverty—or they will defeat us.

There is new hope for a self-renewing transformation of the international community, if we can discard the obsolete notion that toughness translates into security and see instead that true strength can be *shared* between nations. Strength need not be displayed only through conflict between nations; it also can be shared through union and alliance.

We have a long way to go. Visiting the United Nations, one can get the image of children contending in games of manipulation and threat. Along with brilliant negotiating strategies, if we could all bring a little humanity to the table, we might be able to transform and mature the games we play internationally.

The election of a man of moral fiber to the Presidency—a

man who in my opinion is centered enough to really stop the buck at his level and make the truly lonely and difficult decisions himself—may herald an opportunity for the United States to adopt a new role of world leadership. If President Carter has freed himself of the need to earn the approval of everyone, a compulsion which has driven many Presidents to acts of excess and unwisdom, and if he has within himself the inner strength gained through personal growth and spiritual transformation, then this next decade can become an adventure in the transformation of international relationships as we move together to turn our swords into plowshares, and so create a world unity of both tenderness and strength.

After an unprecedented period of scandal and corruption, we may be once again on the threshold of serving as a dynamic force for moral evolution in world society. We Americans are impatient, and we do not like being threatened by others. Yet we have come to realize, largely as a result of Vietnam, that unused nuclear weapons have totally altered the nature of military strategy. The leading military powers have come to see that nuclear weapons are unusable as actual instruments of war —they are too powerful to be used. Their deterrence is a function of their existence, not their use. Nuclear power only makes us the most ferocious-*looking* animal among the many others chained together in the atomic cage. Recent decisions not to invest in an anti-ballistic missile system or the supersonic transport signal a growing realism in our country as to the limits of power. Power without wisdom is terror. And strength without compassion is an invitation to destruction. We must have both if we are to keep either.

This awareness of the need for a more tender way of being is now manifesting itself in terms of our views about world resources. We are beginning to see that tenderness *is* strength when it comes to the conservation of our natural resources. We cannot "rip off" Mother Nature without opening ourselves to the most massive and irreversible disasters. So we are arriving at a point at which a new commitment between nations can be forged to secure for all of us the purity and security of our common natural environment. Just as in our individual relationships with others, interdependence rather than either complete dependence or total independence has become the order of the hour.

Our national struggles for the social and civil rights of all our citizens have also generated a new awareness that can blossom out as an international charter for choice and caring. During his campaign, President Carter said that "the time has come to stop taxing poor people in rich countries for the benefit of rich people in poor countries." This attitude signals the beginning of a new level of compassion and sincerity in strengthening the bonds of humanity which necessarily link the nations of our world.

For more than two hundred years our country has gained more power, more energy, more money, and more "things" than any other nation in history. We are proud—perhaps too proud. Pride leads on to blindness, and blindness on to ruin. It is not only desirable for us to experience a true transformation of our basic orientation toward life, but I believe it is essential for our survival.

Change and the minor adjustments which "change" creates are simply not enough any more. The ocean is dying, we have oil enough only for forty or fifty more years, the air we breathe is filthy, cancer is epidemic, and the earth itself can no longer support the unbridled exponential material "success" of the "American Dream." We are waking up into a nightmare. The cost of our medical care is growing beyond our ability to pay for it, yet we live at only a fraction of our potential. America is ripe for transformation, and it is needed at all levels, from the individual person to the superstructure of our society. We do not need to revolt. We need to evolve.

A journey inward is not, by itself, enough. Our evolution, as individuals and as a nation, must be a combined inward and worldly journey. Our government must exercise the vision and boldness to initiate a program for the full exploration and achievement of our human potentials. Why can we not explore our own space with the same pride and purpose with which we launched men to the moon? Such an Evolution Project could integrate many current programs in health, education, and energy research, so as to activate and actualize the full range of potentials of our minds, bodies, emotions, and spirit.

As a result of the Nixon years our country is permeated with a deep sense of cynicism and even a helplessness. But we are not helpless. We are hurt. The national transformation which is alive below the surface of our pain will manifest itself only as each of us takes full personal responsibility for his life, and for the country's life as a nation: to fight poverty and poor health, drug use and alcoholism, architectural ugliness and mediocrity, bureaucratic waste and inefficiency. We are standing at a crossroads in our national purpose. We are all at risk: the risk of irresponsibility.

Our evolution will require discipline, as unpopular as this concept seems to many today. The kind of discipline we need is not the authoritarian military variety, but rather the beauty of responsible self-discipline in which we enable ourselves to make clear, self-directed choices. From these choices comes our journey toward "a path with heart." Without the heart, there is no path worth traveling. And without discipline, there is no journey, and no strength to choose it.

At present I am working to create an "Olympics" for gifted youth from various nations around the world. This Olympiad will be primarily non-athletic. We already do a great deal for those who display athletic gifts, but far less for those with other gifts. This Olympiad of the mind and senses would bring together teams of future leaders every few years. The assembled youth would participate in intellectual games such as chess and *go*, but also would play non-competitive creativity games never before played and "no lose games" where the purpose would be not to win but to discover more about the minds and feelings of the other players. These young leaders of the future would gather to participate in large-scale simulation exercises in which they would actually work to create solutions to real world issues. Scientific and mathematical/computer fairs would be held. The young musicians on each country's team would perform and artists would exhibit their work. A Festival of Life would be created around the Olympiad to express the true nature and purpose of the event.

In the Catskill Mountains of New York, over the past forty years, Camp Rising Sun has been bringing gifted youth from around the world together to spend summers sharing their customs and mutual curiosity about the youth of other nations. Here some of the values and strengths which will be needed to build a brighter world have been nurtured. George Jonas, the camp's director, is a wise man well into his seventies who travels around the world every year, handpicking gifted and talented teenagers for the following summer's camp. Many of the alumni of this little-known yet highly effective program have now assumed positions of responsibility in their respective countries, and the bonds of trust which they have forged at camp serve them well when the usual diplomatic channels break down. We need more experiments such as this to move our world closer to its source-energies of tenderness and true strength.

14 Tenderness in Birth

> The man who does not believe in miracles surely
> makes it certain that he will never take part in one.
>
> WILLIAM BLAKE

We are now on the frontier of breakthroughs in terms of scientific discoveries and in levels of consciousness that will surely boggle the minds of most of us during the next decade. The work with the DNA and RNA molecules and the genetic implications of this work will raise new moral questions in terms of intelligence and sex determination. New spiritual and intuitive frontiers—previously scorned by scientists and empiricists, left to the so-called fringe groups of courageous parapsychologists or mystics—will soon become acceptable areas for scientific research.

Unexplainable Phenomena

We have evidence from research work done with porpoises that "energy fields" emanating from animals and human beings are real and powerful forces. If you take a porpoise away from its "family group," the remaining porpoises will crash into one another for the next few weeks until they form a new "community." Their energy field is changed with the removal of one of their group. They become a different community and must create new patterns for their energy. The same thing is true of families or classrooms when a teenager leaves for college, or a person dies, or a marriage splits up, or certain children leave a classroom. New social patterns with new energy fields are formed. We sense this intuitively, but we have little hard "proof," so we distrust and dismiss our feelings. We will have to learn to trust and be more open to the subjective data and intuitive feelings which arise in us, rather than awaiting "objective" evidence, which in spiritual matters is not measurable. For some calculations, we need more than machines or computers. We need compassion. We need ourselves.

A Bulgarian psychologist named Georgi Lozonov has developed a method of teaching two years of a foreign language in only six weeks. His instructions to his students? "Lie back in a reclining chair and free your mind from trying to learn." The mind unconsciously opens to more of the incredible potential of its three billion neurons to absorb and retain when a person relaxes in an "alpha state."

I have repeatedly demonstrated before many audiences of skeptical scientists that, merely by focusing my energy out through my forefinger down the front of a person's body from the lower lip to the pubic bone, I literally can take away his strength. Or, by tracing the energy path back up instead of down, I can restore it. Oriental experts have known for years that energy passing down this frontal series of acupuncture points saps strength, while tracing up restores it. Yet we Westerners refuse to open to these so-called unexplainable phenomena. Suddenly the implications of men looking women "down" or "up" are clearer to us.

Joseph Chilton Pearce is a distinguished scholar who has recently made a major effort to take a scientific look at unexplainable phenomena. In his book *The Crack in the Cosmic Egg* he describes the work of scientific teams from both the *National Geographic* and England who studied the fire walkers in Borneo. These scientists confirmed that, though the temperature in the fire pits was over 1400 degrees Fahrenheit, most of the walkers who literally danced barefooted across the smoldering coals had no burns on their bare feet. This was no illusion or trick. These persons, except for the one or two per year who lose faith and do get burned in the middle of the pit, have a "separate reality" awareness of their own which tells their bodies that they will not be burned. How?

Pearce describes student volunteers who in 1966 fasted until their blood sugar was extremely low. They were then hypnotized and fed imaginary bowls of sugar. Immediately, blood samples taken from the students indicated several hundred percent increase in their blood sugar levels. How does this happen?

Aboriginal tribesmen can follow a man leaving no tracks for many miles through the desert by following his energy trail—up to one year after he makes it! The tribes are also able to suddenly pack up camp on a clear dry day and move off in a slow loping jog to intercept rainfall twenty miles away in order to secure their much-needed water. How do they know?

In our Western culture there are so many things to which we allow our intellects to give assent, but so few things which we will allow our souls to affirm. In other cultures, where "separate realities" prevail, quite the opposite is often true. Our toughness often blocks the flow of an intuitive or spiritual awakening which a more natural, tender sense of reality seems to facilitate. And it all begins at the moment of our conception.

Birth Without Violence

African tribeswomen instinctively sing and talk to their fetuses *in utera* from the moment of conception on. Dr. Frederick Leboyer, the French obstetrician who has pioneered the "birth without violence" movement, is bringing babies into the world tenderly in candlelit, music-filled environments, as contrasted with the harshly lit delivery rooms in most hospitals.

From Leboyer's viewpoint, the newborn child is not a *thing* to be dangled upside down, spanked on the rear, wrapped up, and then left in a crib. On the contrary, this new infant is the most exquisitely tender and feeling *being* in the delivery room. We've all been told that the newborn is insensitive to pain and hence won't feel the pain of birth or the cutting of the umbilical cord or the foreskin of the penis in circumcision. These false rationalizations have put mothers' and doctors' minds at ease for too many years. In a Leboyer birth, the child is gently massaged while resting on the mother's warm belly, where her familiar heartbeat can be heard to help the child make the awesome adjustment from the total support of the womb to its new world of increasing independence. After such a rest, the child is bathed in tepid water to calm it after the trauma of birth and to ease the contrast between its new world and the suspended wet darkness of its old world in the womb.

Are there any long-term differences between the development of the "Leboyer baby" and children delivered by conventional methods? A recent study by the French researcher Daniel Rapoport and described in the French journal *Psychologie* suggests that the differences are dramatic. Rapoport tested 120 children—one-, two-, and three-year-olds chosen at random from among a thousand babies delivered by Dr. Leboyer. All the infants scored substantially higher than the average baby on the tests for psychomotor functioning. Even more significant were the comments of their mothers, who came from widely varied backgrounds. They found their children extremely alert, adroit, inventive, and, interestingly, ambidextrous. (Which suggests that our split-brain functioning, with the left lobe usually predomi-. nant, might be traced to the severe ordeal needlessly imposed on the newborn at birth!)

The Leboyer babies walked one to two months earlier than the average infant. One hundred and twelve of the hundred and twenty mothers reported a total absence of "problems" in toilet training and in the child's learning to feed itself. One hundred and seven of the babies had had no digestive or sleeping disorders of any kind. According to Dr. Michel Odent: "Children born in a serene and peaceful way seem to be secure, in their first months, from such psychosomatic symptoms as colic, as well as paroxysmic crying."

Rapoport's research provides the first clinical verification of the theory that birth is the formative experience that we spend the remainder of our lives "working on."

Joseph Chilton Pearce in a lecture given at an Association for Humanistic Psychology convention in 1976 described the contrast between our harsh delivery techniques and the more tender practices of some other cultures. He estimated that fully 40 percent of us suffer brain damage directly resulting from our birth practices.

In the typical American delivery room the mother is anesthetized. The drug is immediately transmitted to the fetus. The child is then delivered (frequently with forceps), and when it needs all its lung function and musculature to make the tremendous adjustment of breathing on its own for the first time, its lungs are handicapped by the anesthetic. To make matters worse, most of our doctors have adopted the practice of immediately cutting the umbilical cord, when for a few precious transition minutes this organ could continue to supply muchneeded oxygen. Under blazing lights the baby is then spanked while being dangled upside down—an apt initiation into the harsh world in which it is to spend its life. Then it has its eyes doused with silver nitrate (just in case the mother has syphilis) before being placed in a nursery crib to cry alone.

Human Bonding

Compare this to the practice of certain African countries where a few minutes before birth the mother stops her work and goes into her hut to deliver her own child. She gets into a squatting position, as compared to our supine, often strapped-down position. She bears her child instinctively, and she tenderly massages the vernix fluid over every inch of the infant while it rests upon her stomach. We're all familiar with the instinctive process the mother cat or dog follows of licking each of her offspring as they are born. If the mother cat misses licking even an area of the stomach, Pearce reports that the kitten will become spastic and will remain so the rest of its life.

After several minutes, when the child's lungs have made the incredible adjustment of taking over the breathing process, the African mother bites through the umbilical cord, and then swaddles the child to her front, where it can feed freely from her breast. (The human infant is naturally a continuous feeder, regardless of our imposed feeding schedules.) In this position, she and her infant can maintain eye contact. She then goes out to show off her new offspring to her friends. Pearce notes that this infant becomes "bonded" to its mother. I have seen photos of these African infants holding up their heads, smiling at their images in a mirror *a few hours after birth!* Our infants, born under an anesthetic in accordance with modern technological procedures, are months behind these African children, who also display superior intelligence during these first years of life.

A researcher observing these African mothers as they stood in line for hours holding their babies and waiting to see the doctor wondered why these undiapered children were not messing on their mothers. The mothers were asked what they did when their children had to eliminate. They indicated that they took them to the bushes. They were then asked how they knew when the child had to go. The mothers laughed and asked the researcher how she knew when she had to go. The truth was that these mothers were so closely bonded to their children that they sensed a subtle tension in their children when their young had to urinate!

Pearce presents the results of research wherein one group of monkeys were born in our usual modern manner, with the mother under anesthetic and the umbilical cord cut immediately after birth. One hundred percent of the monkeys born "our way" suffered brain damage! The slides of their brains revealed obvious damage! In another group of monkeys birthed naturally none of the babies suffered such damage.

I asked Pearce why the African children didn't maintain their head start in intelligence which such a tender and natural beginning had provided them. With such a beginning, one would think they would become a superior adult race. The answer was again a dramatic testimonial to the crucial importance of human tenderness. At age seven the close bond between these children and the mother is abruptly severed, and they are taken away to be reared and trained in another village by strangers. This sudden rupture of the mother-child bond causes a dramatic regressive effect which the child never overcomes.

One of my stepchildren, John, who was born naturally and nursed until he was four, has displayed precociousness in many activities. I am beginning to see that what our grandmothers felt to be true is indeed true—that the more time a child has at the tenderness of the breast, the better off it will be. Plastic bottles create a plastic culture. Instead of being bonded to a human being, our infants are bonded to a crib after birth, in a sterile nursery with blankets or bottles. Perhaps this provides a clue about why our nation is the largest consumer of material goods in the world!

What we lack is passion, the sharing of deep feelings. In an auditorium just after soon-to-be mothers watched a film on natural childbirth, one mother remarked that the sounds of the mother's labor and breathing resembled the ecstatic sounds of orgasm. My wife tells me that the birth of all of her children actually was orgasmic. Childbirth should be passionate. It is only our society's fear of deep feelings which keeps us from those simple discoveries and human joys.

Perhaps, with more attention to tenderness in our environment and in our parenting from conception through birth and early childhood, new and tender human beings can emerge with more of their human potential available. The terrifying, harsh struggle to be born tends to instill in us the imprint that life is a cruel battle in which only the tough and the aggressive will survive. But toughness and aggression are not always strength. They are often masks for our weaknesses and our fears of our lack of strength.

I believe that the Protestant ethic and the old American pioneer spirit, which served us so well in the last century with their dictum that only "a hard life builds character," no longer are relevant to our lives today. Life need not be hard in order to be fully human. If we can begin our lives in a tender fashion, perhaps we will see and experience that the world *is* a beautiful place and that our lives are there to be cared for, not conquered or controlled.

15 Spirituality and Manhood: A Summer Passage

by Gabriel Saul Heilig

Misplaced Worship: Men and Their I-dolls

We tend to think of dolls as ritual toys for little girls, not grown men. One summer I learned otherwise.

I spent part of my summer working in the men's health club at Grossinger's Hotel, the queen of all the resort hotels in New York's Catskill Mountain "borscht belt." I worked as a masseur and rubdown man. While the kitchen staff was working away kneading the dough for Jenny Grossinger's famous rye bread, I was working my way through the doughy flesh of the various mayors, moguls, entertainers, and conventioneers whom Grossinger's attracts. They were rich men, well able to afford the high rates—and many of them rich enough to buy the place outright. Flashing diamond pinky rings and red suede loafers, they ambled into the health club after nine holes out on the links, in for a little sauna and a massage before the evening meal and more of that great rye bread.

Working at Grossinger's gave me an invaluable look behind the well-lacquered veneer of the male ego, and led me to do some thinking about male pride—its pleasures, its pains, and its true costs.

Maleness in America has traditionally been defined in terms of strength, and strength itself has generally been defined in terms of toughness. For all our grade-school genuflections, the classical American hero is *not* Benjamin Franklin or Abraham Lincoln. Our prototype hero is more likely a figure like Billy the Kid: the grinning gunslinger who mows down his enemies without a remorseful wince or the merest whisper of regret. He is "fast," faster than the restraining pull of emotion or of thought. He stands alone, aloof, above the striving and the sway of human emotion. He protects life, but he does not participate *in* life.

Our fast-shooting, slow-talking hero has been updated in recent years, but alterations in his appearance seem to have changed little else in him. He remains the same—decade after decade, movie after movie. He has come to us as: the man in uniform, protecting his country in a jet fighter in a lonely duel at 40,000 feet; the football hero surrounded by a huddle of admiring coeds, but staring past them to some elusive excellence known only on the playing field; the Marlboro Man, totally male and serene atop his horse, somewhere in an unnamed wilderness far from the blaring cities where most American men actually work and live; the Playboy, changing his women as casually as he might change a tape on his eight-track stereo; and the bureaucrat, neatly buttoned down and buttoned up, who seems to have every aspect of his external life under control, but who displays no sign at all of any inner life.

These popular images reveal something to us about ourselves which is disturbing and even a little terrifying. In our gallery of hero imagery there are few hints of softness, tenderness, or spiritual depth. Males appear as perfect pillars of perfect strength. They do not need. They do not change. They do not grow. They are perfect, perhaps, but they are not quite human.

Such hero figures may make powerful idols for little boys to worship, but they make impossible models for young men to emulate. And that is the point. These fantasy images reflect what many men believe we actually want to achieve. This imagery is what we are given to explain to ourselves what manhood *is*. We are raised on these images as boys, graduating from cap-gun fantasies to hot-rodding, *Playboy* machismo, and Monday Night Football. Then, fully programmed, we are pronounced fit for "real life"—where, never having seen much of anything else, we attempt to reproduce these sterile images in our own lives. The tragedy is not that we expend so much energy in the attempt, but that so many of us actually succeed.

America is increasingly populated with such "successes": men who are able to work hard, drink hard, give sex hard, and pull apart the insides of a car; but who are unwilling or simply unable to express and share deep emotions, or to let situations be without somehow having to be on top of them. For too many of us, life's rewards come from conquest, both personal and professional. Our goal in life is to win, but not to share the victory. Yet without celebration victory is hollow. The more we win, the more we are alone.

Instead of sharing our victories and the satisfaction they might bring us, we bask alone in impossible private fantasies: of being undiscovered Supermen, striding fearlessly across the playing fields of life, eluding the tacklers of error, pain, and self-delusion. In our dreams we always score the winning touchdown for our side. But life is longer than a Sunday afternoon.

Many men, perhaps even most of us, think about and seek to actualize ourselves not as persons but as male dolls. We toy with our egos, until *we* become toylike. We worship our self-concepts, but we fail to honor ourselves. The result of worship-

ing the idols of male imagery is that we turn *ourselves* into dolls,
by way of imitation. Image becomes idol. Idol becomes I-doll.
And somewhere in this process the "I" is lost. We focus on the
objects of our worship, forgetting the one inside us who does the
worshiping.

It is not long before our lives are commanded by these images
of who we think we are or ought to be—an insulting thought,
perhaps, yet an accurate one if we are to judge by the images of
American manhood we see arrayed before us daily in the mass
media. The American male depicted in the mass media *is* very
much like a doll. He has his dress-up kit by Colgate or Cardin,
depending on his income bracket, and he has his add-on male
attachments: his attaché case or hard hat, as the case may be, his
"personal luxury" car and CB radio, his push-button electronic
watch, his credit cards, and his favorite beer.

My description is a caricature, of course. And yet I have the
uneasy feeling that the number of American men who seek to
fulfill the pattern these images describe is actually quite high.
There is a distinct and not-so-subtle pressure on American men
to live out today's chapter of the "American Dream": *having*
all of these things, without having to do anything *about* them,
except to use them once in a while as a way of claiming one's
ownership. It is a bourgeois picture of what life ought to be. A
paradise of possession. A carnival of consumption. But all without very much aliveness. The ego is fed, and then overfed. But
the person inside the I-doll is treated more like a stranger than
a guest. While the I-doll is served, he starves.

We pretend we are Playboys. We like to imagine that
women are as available as the nearest light switch, and as easily
turned on. Every Playboy assumes that he is "in control." He
wants his women to be hot, but he is definitely "cool." What he
fails to notice is that he is actually a sucker for every seller in
the male-image business. They run him. He is their creation,
their little I-doll to dress (and undress) as they please. Whenever

they want to change him, they simply change the fashion line, and out their I-doll goes to shop for a new wardrobe. The Playboy turns out to be a doll—a grown-up male doll for men who suppose they are too tough and too smart to ever be caught playing with dolls.

In fact, of course, few men actually experience a life as uncomplicated or unreal as in their adolescent fantasies. Most of us do hurt inside now and then. We do doubt ourselves. The women *we* know aren't waiting for us like so many velour-lined slippers. They are just as likely to throw their slippers *at* us.

Another aspect of America's male I-doll worship is worth noting: Almost without exception, this imagery is focused *outside the self.* The football hero and the lone gunslinger, the Marlboro Man and the Playboy (and his black counterpart, Superfly), all seek their satisfactions *outside* themselves. None look within. The pantheon of American fantasy heroes is virtually devoid of any hint of spirituality, reflection, or even intellectual prowess, for that matter. "Eggheads" and "smartypants" are not well loved in our country. We do not trust our geniuses. We honor them and we envy them, perhaps, but we also usually find ways to make them pay for being smarter than the rest of us.

And beyond the mind there is the heart. The heart. For most American men, the heart is off limits. Sex, money, and power are the male agenda—not love, and certainly not the life of the spirit. A "liberated" man can explore every avenue of sexual adventure without much comment today, but any open talk of spirituality is taboo. In America today, for many people, the true dirty word is "God."

Inside the I-doll: The Being in the Body

It is as though we all walk through the world carrying a Secret. It is an open Secret, one we all share. What we share is a Life which unites and binds and entwines us throughout our lives here on earth, whether we prefer to think so or not. It is simply one of the conditions of our lives that we be Alive. There is no other way around it. We are all Alive.

But alas, we live now in a culture and in a time in which simply *being* is not enough. Our society asks us to go beyond being. It moves us subtly, constantly, and very persuasively in the direction of *doing* and *having*. It does not matter much precisely *what* we are doing or having, as long as we *are* doing and having. It is not "American" simply to be. For to be becomes to Be; and if people were content to Be, our economy might falter, since so much of it is based on the purchasing of luxury and illusion. Why buy illusions when one can have the real thing free? It is a question Madison Avenue would rather we didn't ask.

To choose one obvious and omnipresent example, the media do an excellent job of selling us our own sexuality. Media advertising does not encourage us to *experience* our sexuality. For to do that, all we have to do is be. Part of what we *are* is sexual. Rather, the media attempt to move us in the direction of believing sexuality is something we lack and need to possess. And the way to do that, of course, is to buy it.

The result is that we wind up purchasing what we already have—and are. Perfume, clothing, cars, cologne, even toothpaste—could anything possibly be less sexy than cleaning one's teeth? Obviously (or not so obviously), it isn't the advertised item that provides the innuendoed sexual energy. *We* provide that. What is being sold is not an item but an idea. Yet it is we who hold the consciousness which brings these ideas to life. We give *them* life, and it is not, as the media would have us believe, the items and ideas we buy which give life and aliveness to us.

Still the myth prevails—that life is outside us and we have to get it. To buy it. To hoard it. To keep it from escaping. The myth is empty, yet we prop it up by our frenzied rush to consume everything we can.

I think we have it backward. It is *we* who produce life, *we* who create aliveness and value in the world around *us*. Our media-manipulated fear of not *having* enough blinds us to how much we *are* within ourselves. There are few inventions of technology which are not merely imitations of innate human powers. Computers can perform complex logical operations, yet they cannot intuit. Airplanes need immense amounts of fuel to fly. We do it every night when we dream, and it costs us nothing. The telephone is enormously useful, but hardly a match for ESP and other forms of direct intuitional communication. Color television can be fun, but it too pales beside the panorama we all hold inside us, if we simply take the time to shut our eyes in silence and look at it. What we are is so much greater than anything we possibly could have. Yet still the myth prevails.

Why?

Alan Watts once wrote a book which he subtitled *The Taboo Against Knowing Who You Are*. There is part of an answer there, I think. Our society, like almost every other, is eager to teach its members who we *ought* to be. That bends us toward obedience. The other side of this tendency toward insuring behavioral predictability is that our society also works subtly to keep us ignorant about who we actually *are*. If we knew, we might be a lot less docile than we are now.

One obvious and current example of this has been the sudden overturning of perceptions and attitudes that has resulted from the feminist movement. For years all of us (especially men) assumed we knew what women were. They were . . . women. And everyone knew, or supposed he knew, what that meant. Now we are not so certain about our traditional pictures of what "women" are supposed to be or do. There is no common agreement yet as to what any *new* definition might be, yet even our uncertainty about the *old* definition has produced a dramatic shift in values and behavior. Such is the power of paradigms and mental imagery—and of women.

Contemporary psychologists are only now beginning to explore what may be there behind the common assumptions almost all of us unquestioningly make about what a "human being" actually is, or can be. Who *are* we, really? How many of us truly feel that we know? Yet for all our doubts about these fundamental questions, how righteous and cocksure we often are in telling others who *they* ought to be. Husbands tell wives. Parents tell children. We all tell each other. But what do we really know?

It is ironic that in a society which apparently values nothing more highly than individualism, the actual condition is one of mass mirror-imagery. In clothing and housing, in vocabulary and slang styles, in diets and diversions—even in our vices—we are a society struggling desperately to be alike. One might almost conclude that we were reacting to a deeply felt need to acknowledge an impulse to be at one with one another. But that would be to give away part of our Secret, and we are not yet ready to let on that we know that much. So the myth prevails. And with it the paradox: that in a society which was founded to assure religious freedoms, we still feel inhibited to explore and to express our spirituality.

For men in particular this inhibition takes a dangerous turn. Our refusal to openly experience our softer emotions or to express our higher impulses leads us to over-rely on and to over-emphasize our harder, "masculine" emotions. Our emotional as well as our physical arteries begin to harden. In order for any feeling at all to penetrate, it must be progressively more exaggerated. We turn strength into toughness, and we parody manhood into machismo. We are no longer men. We are "tough guys."

Ordinarily we think of toughness as being the opposite of weakness, and roughly the same as strength. Yet toughness is quite different from true strength. It is different in much the same way that apathy is different from either love or hate. Just as apathy negates both love *and* hate by blocking any feeling at all, so toughness prevents us from experiencing either strength or weakness. Weakness is a lack of energy. Strength is the free flow of energy in abundance. Toughness, on the other hand, is energy which has been walled up inside itself in one rocklike posture. Strength increases aliveness. Toughness shuts it down. Machismo is a caricature, a cartoonlike posture we force the world to accept; yet once committed to it, we are also forced to ante up on our own bluff. The sad result is that the natural flow of strength which is part of manhood becomes locked inside the macho pose. Statues are not strong. They are only hard.

Men and women both, we are caught inside the same illusion, although we struggle alone on opposite sides of it. Our costumes and our scripts, our attitudes and acts, may be different, yet our illusion is identical. The illusion is that we *are* dolls, unable to shape our lives ourselves, and unable to create our lives out of ourselves. The message in the media everywhere we turn is that we are not Beings but merely bodies. As bodies, all we can do is live life from the outside in. And so every day we are flooded with hundreds of promptings urging us to pamper our smiles and suntans, our hairdos and our complexions. What is missing, of course, is any interest in what lies beneath these doll-like superficialities. For many of us it isn't long before we begin to identify with the faces we see in our mirrors, and not with the light inside them. We soon lose interest in what else there may be to us besides our clothes and our accessories. And eventually we forget about it altogether.

What we forget is who we are. What we remember is who we have been taught to be.

From Symbol to Source: A Summer Passage

How do we find our way out of this spiritual dead-end—particularly when our society encourages us to rush down this blind alley as fast as we can?

For most of my own life, I had groped around for answers. For many years, books were an answer. I can recall how one day as an undergraduate I stood in the midst of the open stacks of the college library thinking that if only I could read all the books in the literature section, I would be home free. Life would ask nothing more of me than my dog-eared library card. But Life was interested in more than my reading list.

After graduation, it came home to me. Afraid, unprepared, I married and soon divorced. Confused, I wandered through the arms of more women than I could hold or love. I opened the door of drugs, and went in. I learned a great deal, and broke through to a state of consciousness in which I could feel my innate power as a Being. Yet, unable to integrate these experiences in my daily living, I kept re-entering the same door.

Finally my life began to break apart. I left a good job as director of a ten-college project. I left one relationship with a woman after another. I left my friends confused and my parents concerned. I knew I was more than the sum total of my raging frustrations—and in the end, out of these frustrations, a breakthrough occurred. My I-doll broke open, and I broke free.

In my thirty-third summer the lonely autumn of my adolescence ended and I entered the bright spring of my maturity. Every afternoon, after leaving the massage tables at Grossinger's, I would hitchhike back to South Fallsburg, where two friends and I had rented a bungalow just down the road from the DeVille Hotel. Once the proud Nemerson Hotel, its name when my parents had vacationed there years ago, the DeVille had long since run out of borscht and bagels and had fallen on lean times. In the spring of 1976 it had been rented for five months to serve as the summer ashram of Swami Muktananda Paramahansa.

Swami Baba Muktananda was concluding a two-and-a-half-year tour through North America. Almost alone among the numerous healers, mahatmas, "gurus," and sub-gurus who had journeyed to the West, Muktananda had been accepted virtually without dissent as a genuine master of consciousness by those who might be supposed to constitute his primary competition in the "spiritual supermarket." The Indian government had actually issued an official proclamation declaring him to be a living saint, the only time it had taken such an unusual step. I decided that Muktananda had more than the standard run of paisley p.r. to offer. I arranged to spend five months at his ashram.

Every afternoon after work I would walk over to the DeVille to participate in the evening program at the ashram. The hotel had been thoroughly transformed from a transient pleasure palace into a floating opera of inner attainment. Over the front door hung a huge hand-painted sign: "God dwells in you as you. See God in each other." As the months passed, the message on the sign became less a slogan and more an insistent demand. Once through the door to Muktananda's consciousness, there was no way back out. There was only forward.

Thankfully, there was nothing especially exotic or elaborate about the ashram programs. Every evening several hundred of us would sit in the great meditation hall and chant. The hall itself, which was used for no other purpose than chanting and meditation, was the power source and psychic caldron of the ashram. We would chant for twenty minutes, and then Muktananda would enter the hall. He would lead us in a chant of the mantra which had been passed down through the entire and

ancient lineage of Siddha Yoga, of which he was now the living
master. The mantra was not secret; its only secret was its power.
Then Muktananda would greet each of us individually, swatting
us gently with his scepter of peacock feathers as double lines of
people passed before him. Then he would spend half an hour
answering written questions from us, giving immediate and
telling answers that seemed to speak directly to each unnamed
questioner. "Baba, I love God so much, but I don't know where
to find Him. I look and look. What should I do?" Baba: "Don't
go looking for God. God is always looking for *you*."

And then he would meditate with us. That was always the
climax and resolution. A plaintive Indian melody would float
like incense through the great hall as we sat there lost in some
tiny fraction of Muktananda's inner world. There is no way to
describe fully what I imbibed in those simple afternoons with
Muktananda. He has influenced my life profoundly—of that I
have no doubt. Nor do I any longer have any desire to resist the
process of inner unfoldment which that summer's audience
with him began. As my awareness of his teaching has deepened,
I have learned to welcome the surrender of my ego: to him, to
my new family and the many people in my life, and to the
unspiraling of my own spirit.

What Muktananda taught us was so utterly simple it sounds
almost banal to repeat it: "Meditate on your Self, worship your
Self, kneel to your Self, remember your Self. Whatever is yours
is in you. Always remember this."

"God dwells within you *as* you," he would tell us. "Enter
your own heart and learn to roam there. The Self is pure consciousness. It is not your body, and not your mind. It is neither
male nor female. It is beyond physical condition, sensation,
thought, or gender. The Self is not the manifestations of consciousness. It is their source. Find that source within yourself,
for that is where it is."

The longer I spent with Muktananda, the more deeply this truth opened my awareness. The human body joins us to a world of manifest reality. That world is huge, yet it is limited —as is the body's ability to join with it. Yet within the body there is another world, at least as vast and more available. The body itself is small, yet within the body the Self is free and without size. It is not bound by mind or body, birth or death. It is always source: source-point to our motions in the mortal world of darkening time.

"The body is like a theater," Muktananda would say. "It is the theater in which you experience the world. Your senses are the spectators. Do not let them direct the action."

As my meditations deepened, I began to experience what Baba had been telling us. At times my body would suddenly fill with light, and I would be left breathless as my physical being seemed to energize itself from a source deep within it. At other times I would experience my awareness outside my body altogether, as if guiding and monitoring it. Gradually I began to experience a growing sense of space within myself. When my eyes and senses were turned outward toward the world, the world seemed very large and I seemed very small. Yet when I shut my eyes and turned my senses inward, the world that awaited me then seemed endlessly huge and inviting. Within myself there opened a limitless source of space and light. Through the guidance of Muktananda I had been led to my own source-energies.

Nothing was required to reach the source-point but to sit quietly in meditation and allow my mind to steep itself in them. What a relief to immerse my mind in the refreshing bliss of thought-less light after so many years of mental fizz. Instead of being given the results of my mind, I was now able to move beyond them to its source: consciousness. Where once meditation had seemed like an impossible and annoying chore—having to "sit still" for so long while my mind chattered away about everything in my life—now the daily meditation sessions became a source of joy and amazement. Sitting quietly, doing nothing (as the Taoist saying goes), I was taken to the most extraordinary places.

I began to see that this lesson applied throughout my life, not only when I sat in meditation. Like the musk deer which runs in a crazed frenzy through the forest seeking the scent which emanates from its own body, how often *I* had searched to find what I already possessed. I began to see that the love and satisfaction I had sought for so long sat quietly within *me*, waiting to be admitted to my consciousness as the sources of my strength, not as the prizes of any power I might ever gain. At long last I had found my own way out of the prison of male pride. The inward path I had been set upon by Muktananda had been available to me all along. I had simply never bothered to seek my freedom in the one place where it always could be found—within myself.

The inward path is not one which American males traditionally have chosen to follow. It seems too inactive, too boring. That is how it *seems*, not how it *is*. For it offers to us the completion we have sought in the ego's endless clamor for claim and conquest. It *is* a way out—not a dead end.

Symbol or source: the choice is always there. I-dolls have no eyes; they can see no light. They have no minds, can think nothing new. They have no hands, can feel no warmth or pain or tenderness. And they have no hearts. I-dolls are phantoms of the ego's struggle to control what it cannot be: images to whose size we reduce ourselves so that we may worship them. Yet, just as we have sacrificed our aliveness on these altars of ego worship, so we also can renew our inner strength and draw closer to its source as we withdraw our attention and energy from the I-dolls of our imagined liberation. We have fashioned these

I-dolls, and they have nearly destroyed us. Now we must re-own and re-enter our own selves.

What bars our way? I think it is our pride—our pride that we have conquered manhood and left behind forever our fear of unknown spaces. We have conquered space and planted flags upon the moon, yes—but not yet roots within the waiting mystery of our own being. We still tremble before the Self like children before the falling dark.

Once we have dared to make our passage inside the heart, we will find that we have entered into a world in which depth leads on to light, and there is no end to entrance. As my summer wore on, the more I surrendered and let my spirit lead me, the more space I experienced within myself in meditation, and the more I saw that I could re-create this space *outside* me in my life in the world. The more I honored Muktananda, the more I saw him as simply a reflection of my own inner nature. I began to see him not as an exotic foreigner, nor as a superior being, but as one who had so totally immersed his ego in his inner Self that he was now completely and immediately connected to his entire universe—and therefore also to me.

Still, Muktananda's teachings were so simple and unvarying that it was hard to keep my mind from wandering away from them. Gradually, as the summer months passed, I became more deeply absorbed in the unavoidable and inevitable wisdom of his teaching. When at times I became lost in the myriad games of my ego, I now found that I could "stop the world" and see beyond these ego-reinforcing states to a level of consciousness which was somehow at the same time both primordial and perfect. At these moments my ego's moods and its mental chatter would disappear, and I would experience the clarity and inner calm of which Muktananda spoke.

"Your Self already is perfect and pure," he had told us. "It is complete. All that is incomplete is your understanding of who you are."

As the weeks and months led summer into fall, I was able to observe myself with greater equanimity. I could see how obvious and ridiculous my posturing and poses were, and how much they simply restricted me. Again and again, I was forced to see how I repeatedly acted out the limited roles which my limited mind had prepared for me. I watched in amazed fascination as I would reach out for the world's attention—only to lose my own.

I began to see my ego for what it was: a psychological attic filled with old games and dolls that begged to be taken out and played with once again. Gradually I saw that I did not have to live there any more. Muktananda showed me that there was a huge mansion awaiting me, once I chose to leave the attic.

16 Tenderness in Dying

> But today he only saw one of the river's secrets, one
> that gripped his soul. He saw that the water continually
> flowed and flowed and yet it was always there; it was
> always the same and yet every moment it was new.
> HERMANN HESSE, SIDDHARTHA

Tenderness can ennoble our leaving of our bodies and this
world in the process of death, just as it can enhance our entering
the world through a gentle birth. In recent years much reputa-
ble research has been done by psychologists and psychiatrists
studying "near death" experiences of patients and accident
victims who clinically had been declared dead. Miraculous
recoveries of persons who have been pronounced medically
dead are not uncommon.

Near-Death Experiences

One of the leading authorities on the dimensions of terminal
illness is the psychiatrist Dr. Elisabeth Kubler-Ross, who has in
her writings and lectures described the psychological stages of
the process of death commonly experienced by those who know
they are dying. These stages are denial, anger, bargaining, and

finally transformation from dying to a more joyful life beyond death. Dr. Kubler-Ross has been criticized by some of her colleagues for departing from the "objectivity" of empirical data for the subjectivity of her intuitive leaps of faith. Yet there are certain common positive experiences described by *all* of Dr. Kubler-Ross's subjects, and by others who have experienced near-death situations. Among these are a sense of peace, wholeness, and a detachment from or a leaving of the physical body. One of her patients, who was blind, during a "miraculous recovery" was able to describe in precise detail everything that took place around him in one such a near-death experience. Other people report meeting previously lost loved ones. Often there is described an episode of being drawn toward a bright light, which, according to some of those experiencing the phenomenon, is described as God or love. They report a sense of being filled with the knowledge that if they went to the light they would leave their bodies behind them and would not return. Accordingly, death need not necessarily be considered the end of our relationships—or of our consciousness.

Several of these individuals report the experience of leaving their physical bodies and watching the scene while actually hovering above their bodies. Others report an increase in the power of their minds and an ESP communication capability. Several centers, including one at the University of Virginia Medical Center and another at Stanford Research Institute, are committed to doing further research on near-death and death experiences.

One professional, Dr. Raymond Moody, recently interviewed fifty people who had come very close to death but had recovered. Dr. Moody's research reinforces that of Dr. Kubler-Ross. The near-death experiences of all of his subjects, though unique for each patient, contained several common elements. Each had an experience of leaving the body, followed by relief, peace, and quiet. Several patients described "heavenly music," and most felt a sense of traveling rapidly through a tunnel, emerging at the end to find themselves actually witnessing their own death scenes. They were able to accurately describe technical procedures and events which took place during their unconscious near-death trips! Several attempted unsuccessfully to communicate with their doctors or others at their death scenes. They had the consciousness necessary for such communication, but not the physical instrument. Perhaps one day we will learn how to communicate directly—consciousness to consciousness.

The Ultimate Light

These persons also reported experiencing greatly enhanced intellectual powers, as if the mind, once freed of physical limitations and restrictions, were able to soar to incredible new heights and powers. Many of these near-death patients described non-verbal encounters with spiritual "helpers," who were often deceased friends or family members. The most common experience described by nearly all of Dr. Moody's patients was the emergence of bright "light," often in the form of God, an angel, or other *heavenly* being who radiated warmth and love.

This event usually preceded a rapid and accurate autobiographical review of the individual's life. The individual was then faced with a decision of whether or not to go to the tempting light, knowing that if he went he would never return to his body, as each of these interviewed patients obviously chose to do. The element of choice is apparently very much a factor in the decisions of a dying person. Small wonder that so many who have experienced a long and painful illness elect tenderly to let go and pass on to the light.

The questions of the separation of the soul from the body
and the soul surviving the body in an afterlife become a very
real issue. Those who have had near-death experiences inevitably claim that they are no longer afraid of dying, since they
know that death can be the most beautiful of experiences.

The experience of death can be facilitated by the families of
the dying. The terminally ill should not be left to die in sterile
hospital environments or be deprived of all the pleasures that
once enriched their lives, such as their children, good food,
hobbies, music, and the familiar surroundings of the home.
They should be encouraged to go home or to favorite settings.
It is painfully clear that our hospitals do not provide happy
environments for the sick or the dying. Rather than hiding from
the experience of death, the dying can participate in planning
their own funerals or ceremonial arrangements, deciding who
will attend, what activities should take place, what music should
be played. Dr. Kubler-Ross suggests that in the final months of
their lives the dying can have a fulfilling experience of giving
away their prized possessions to special people.

Death need not be viewed as a permanent separation from
loved ones, but as a temporary leave-taking. If this leave is
taken tenderly, rather than in a desperate fight to survive, it can
become the ultimate experience and transformation for each of
us.

The Death of My Mother

When I contrast this attitude toward dying with the one that
I experienced at my mother's deathbed, I conclude that I want
my dying to be different. My mother was dying from a painful
breast cancer which had spread throughout her body. She was
in an oxygen tent when I arrived, summoned from my studies
at West Point during her final hours. I had never been told that
she was dying.

Somehow she had so much more wisdom than the rest of us. She unzipped the oxygen tent to hold my hand, over the protest of the nurses and other attendants around her. In my "positive thinking" and insensitive manner, I tried optimistically to reassure her she would recover and be well again. She knew better. I would not admit that she was dying. Because of my stubborn narrow-minded viewpoint, I missed forever telling her how much she really meant to me as my mother, how much her presence meant to me as a child when my father was away during World War II, how much I loved her. I deprived both her and myself of the sharing of these tender feelings and meanings. And yet there *was* plenty of advance time to prepare for her death. She knew she was terminally ill with cancer.

In another very personal experience with death, I learned once again about the importance of mourning the loss of someone special.

My first-born child, a little girl, Kimberly, died a few days after her premature birth. She was large enough, almost four pounds, but she just stopped breathing, unpredictably, as is sometimes the case with premature babies. The Army doctor at the Fort Campbell hospital had no real explanation for this, and though we requested an autopsy, we never received it or any adequate explanation. This was a crushing blow to us— easier on me, perhaps, than on my wife. A wise old Army nurse who had a great deal of experience with life and death, and who apparently knew how out of touch military men often are with their feelings, called me into a back room at the hospital and told me that my baby was a beautiful baby and suggested that it might be easier for me to mourn if I had the chance to hold her once in my arms. She presented me with my lost child wrapped in a blanket. She uncovered the precious but lifeless little face, which resembled my father's—even his red hair— and left me in the room for a while to allow my grief to surface, which it immediately did. From this surrendering, I found the strength to carry me through the loss of my child.

When people learn that they are dying and accept the fact, they tend to become more sensitive and aware. Unfortunately, when they need so much more touch, intimacy, and sensitivity, we tend to give them just the opposite—treating them as though death were a contagious disease.

Close family members especially fear the pain of accepting the imminent loss of a loved one, often leaving most communication up to acquaintances, nurses, and doctors, who are really inadequate substitutes for loved ones in such time of need. Both loved ones and physicians (who are trained to prolong life) need to be facilitated or trained in "letting go," in order that the dying may die tenderly and peacefully. Physical surroundings for people to die in need to be beautiful and naturally peaceful, conducive to letting go rather than hanging on.

If You Had One Month to Live . . .

Imagine for a moment that you have just been told by your doctor that you have only a month left to live. How would you spend that time? Where would you go? What would you say to the different special people—loved ones, family, friends—in your life? These are the important, often unsaid things. Let me suggest that you close this book now and really imagine that you have only one month more. Make a list of things you would do and say to special people. If you value living here and now, over the next month *do* some of those things—and insure that you create space to share with your special people these truly important communications. You may find your life and theirs enriched in *this* world.

Recently, after reading Aldous Huxley's novel *Island,* I then read a description of his first wife's death. Huxley had actually used the tender techniques to ease his own wife's death which he later described in this novel. He used hypnotism to enable his wife to enjoy food and nourishment long after she otherwise would have. He soothed and talked to her about letting go when the time was appropriate. He helped her to experience her death with dignity and tenderness. Huxley's second wife, Laura, writes in a later book, *This Timeless Moment,* about Huxley's own death, which also was tender. Several hours before his death he had a physician friend administer the hallucinogenic drug LSD to him to facilitate his letting go. His death became a final, integrating spiritual experience.

Death can be this for all of us—if we are willing to accept it as simply another step forward on a personal journey. Between ourselves and the beyond there stands the inevitable door of death. It is a door we all must open and pass through. Usually we fear it. We have been taught to fear it. Yet perhaps our picture of death as an endless blank nothingness is not accurate. Perhaps, as Dr. Kubler-Ross and Dr. Moody are discovering from their interviews of those who have been brought back from near-death incidents, the actual experience of death is something which is both beautiful and painless. Perhaps, as Walt Whitman wrote in *Leaves of Grass,* "to die is different from what everyone supposed—and luckier."

Loneliness

Loneliness is a basic emotion, yet we are conditioned to deny it and to fear it. For me, my own despair and loneliness have become an anchor holding me to my genuineness as a human being. To the degree that I experience my loneliness fully within myself, I become and am alive. It is my experience of my here-and-now loneliness—the fact that I *am* ultimately alone—which enables me to realize how much I really appreciate, love, and value my own uniqueness and that of the other persons in my life.

In the book *Seven Arrows* by Hyemeyohsts Storm, I learned

that in the Cheyenne Indian culture there is the belief that the one way in which all "the People" are created equal is in their loneliness. We all share what can be a powerful bond of loneliness at times in our lives. It is this which makes loving another human being such a precious act.

Earning our approval from others instead of from within ourselves, reacting to please others instead of acting to please ourselves, sets in motion an alienating process that causes us to grow further and further away from our deepest feelings. We become numb, alienated from our feelings and our bodies, when we play such roles. And yet it is so hard not to succumb to the temptation to conform. Society rewards us for doing its tough things, yet chastises us for marching to our own tender heartbeat.

I am only now beginning to appreciate the intense fear, isolation, and loneliness that I avoided as a child. How desolate and despairing it was to be beaten up by other children! This occurred frequently to me, the new kid who changed schools on the average of twice a year. And how alone I was, not sharing my broken heart and fears with my mother, in order not to burden her. I was so sure I wasn't worthy of causing her any trouble. She had enough troubles, I thought, with Dad away and her own illness. How wrong I was! If only I had told her how lonely I was, perhaps we could have grown closer. She might have revealed to me the intenseness of her own loneliness, and in the painful sharing we might have grown closer.

I deeply regret that I never shared with her the poignancy of our mutual loneliness. At her deathbed, fifteen years later, by avoiding reality—by being the positive thinker—I missed my last chance to bridge the chasm of our solitude. Thus we were both denied the true meaning and essence of what we meant to each other.

I don't want to be denied that vital experience in the name

of "positive thinking" when *I* am dying. I want those who love me to be real—so we may share openly what we have meant to each other, and not deny forever the full experiencing of the loss we will suffer when we lose one another.

This true deep experiencing of here-and-now loneliness is very different from the fear of being alone. The fear of being rejected by others or society is a symptom of our "stuckness" in environmental support rather than the centered state of growing to self-support.

The loneliness I experienced after separating from my wife and children was probably my first deep exploration into the rich but frightening chasm of my inner self. One of the most painful parts of this experience was the sense of loss I felt at being cut off from my two young sons, with whom I felt so very close. At that time my own pain emerged on the surface first as deep concern for them. But I have since discovered that it was also very much concern for myself—my own devastating loneliness.

I often experience an intense feeling of loneliness in "official" social settings. I recall a cocktail party in an elegant State Department dining room in Washington, D.C., where I felt utterly alone among several hundred people all engaged in small talk. As I looked across the room at the small clusters of people, most of them gathered around various dignitaries who were spouting their "approved solutions," I felt a chill of loneliness shudder through my body. I realized that the dignitaries were perhaps even lonelier than I. Cocktail parties can be almost as lonely as new schools.

The loneliness that follows divorce is perhaps the most painful experience a child will ever experience, and with so many marriages in this country now ending in divorce, many more children will have to face it. Yet it is vital to let the child experience it deeply—to lead him tenderly through the experience of it, to let him know that it is healthy and allowable to cry about it. Only then will life emerge anew; only then will the people involved realize how much they mean to one another, rather than simply feeling nothing—which the constant avoidance of loneliness virtually insures.

Being with a friend who is dying is an intensely lonely experience. Openly facing both your feelings of loneliness and fear, giving to each other the deep experience of what you mean to each other, is necessary then. It is important not to waste those precious hours in idle talk or wishful thinking. When you value someone, what a deprivation it is to avoid the essence of what you really mean to each other!

When I have been in this situation, I have openly wrestled with my need to say beautiful, clever, or poetic-sounding things; but instead of composing cognitive lines, I allow myself to blunder in my confusion. I think that I communicate more in my confusion than ordered words could ever convey.

At other times I tap into my loneliness—on an airplane, perhaps, or in my office—and often tears start. From somewhere deep within, the sap of life flows, and I feel tender and real. Then an alive, solid, strong feeling arises from within me. For me this is a powerfully rejuvenating process.

Clark Moustakas has written two beautiful books on loneliness, entitled *Loneliness* and *Loneliness and Love,* in which he openly reveals his essence as he explains his own loneliness. He literally immersed himself in loneliness, researching it from his own experience. He calls this process "heuristic" or "phenomenological" research, experiencing something prior to reading about it. He felt that to read about loneliness before experiencing it might contaminate his experience of it.

He steeped himself in a lonely and moving experience involving a decision for open-heart surgery for his daughter. He visited lonely children in hospitals who had been abandoned by their parents because of emergency situations or terminal ill-nesses. He watched as they rebelled against abandonment while the nurses sugar-coated these children's real feelings in order to maintain the false tranquillity of the hospital setting. Gradually the children quieted down and became "well ad-justed": passive and apathetic, their loneliness and fears stuffed deep down inside them.

Moustakas would talk with these youngsters and help them to open their feelings of loneliness and pain. Their quiet grief would be broken, and their agony would burst into tears and cries as they owned and experienced the grief that was right-fully theirs. For these children this was a vital first step back to reality—back to their own essence and healthier living. Though they usually caused the nurses more trouble with their disrup-tive aliveness, they were human beings rather than numb, con-tained robots. Moustakas went on to interview other lonely people: old people sitting out their twilight years on park ben-ches, people rejected by society. Rather than reading other studies of loneliness, which he saved until last in his research process, he read biographies of lonely people like Alger Hiss and Benedict Arnold who were totally rejected by friends and society.

Out of his own experience, his book *Loneliness* evolved. In it, he concludes that

There is a power in loneliness, a purity, self-immersion and depth, which is unlike any other experience. Being lonely involves a certain pathway, requires a total submersion of self, a letting be of all that is and belongs, a staying or remaining with the situation, until a natural realization or completion is reached; when a lonely existence com-pletes itself, the individual becomes, grows from it, reaches out for others in a deeper, more vital sense.*

*Clark Moustakas, *Loneliness* (Englewood Cliffs, N.J.: Spectrum Books, 1961).

There is both an exquisite tenderness and the strength that invariably accompanies it in true loneliness. Our willingness to experience this basic fact and emotion, one which unites us all in its silent bond, is truly part of the wisdom of life, and the dignity of dying.

Flowing Toward Tenderness Through Dream

While on my annual vacation in New Hampshire we always visit a beautiful spot in the White Mountains on the slopes leading to majestic Mount Washington. A crystal-clear cold stream makes its way down the mountain, and at this special place where our family stops to skinny-dip in the freezing water, a waterfall rushes over a boulder. I always crawl up under the waterfall to the small cave which is hidden behind the cascade.

Recently, I had a dream about being in that cave when suddenly the rocks came roaring down, trapping me beneath them. Though the rocks didn't crush me, search and search as I would I could find no opening large enough to squeeze out. As the cold water from the stream began to flow through my prison beneath the rocks, I would go in and out of panic, realizing that I might drown. Then I would calm down and logically try to think of a way out. I imagined my wife and family outside trying to rescue me in vain. The boulders were too huge to move.

It was miles down the mountain to where any cranes or bulldozers might be found, and even if they came, the stream was in a small canyon inaccessible to them. If the dozers or cranes did make it, moving the boulders would more than likely crush me. There was nothing they could do and very little, it seemed, that I could do. I searched my small tomb in vain for ways to squeeze through the boulders and the small cracks of light I longed to pass through. I was cold and wet and panicked again and again as claustrophobia replaced logic. I passed in and out, in and out, between terrifying helplessness and struggle, searching for a logical solution.

Finally, I awoke in a pool of sweat, all tangled up in the sheets. I shared my terror with Eta, and finally realized after basking in the safety of her arms for a while that I *was* free, that I was not really trapped beneath the rocks, except in my dream.

But dreams are real. They contain our uncontaminated inner feelings. They represent the pure stuff. Dreams do not pay any attention to inhibitions, society, or "shoulds." They are uncontaminated by all the conventions of socialization, and for this reason they contain important rich messages for us, if we can decipher them.

One way of working on dreams, taught by the late Fritz Perls, is to become each of the people or things in your dream, one by one, actually getting into the role of each. I did that with this dream of mine.

First I became trapped beneath the rocks: "I must find a way out! I am trapped! At least the rocks did not crush me, but if they had snuffed out my life, I would not need to suffer such terror and pain!"

Rational me takes over again: "Can they get me out from outside? No. Too far for help. Dozers couldn't get down here and they'd crush me if they did. I am helpless and no one else can help me."

Then I became one of the boulders: "I am cold and hard. I am heavy. He is trapped beneath me. I am not alive. I am numb. He is alive, but he is trapped beneath me. I cannot think. I am just heavy and hard and cold and unalive. He cannot move me. But he is clever and if he escapes, he must use his cleverness. I have no cleverness. I am just here. But he cannot manipulate or move me. He cannot fight me. He must find other ways."

Then I became the water flowing through: "I am the cold water. I am not trapped, because I flow through. I do not panic. I flow. I am cold, but I support life in my flow. I can show him how to flow. He can follow me."

And then me again: "The water is right. It flows. It does not panic. I can flow with it. It can lead me out as it flows out. I can flow. The water does not battle the rocks, as I was doing, but flows with and through them. If I live, it will be because I flow out with the water as the water flows. If I die, I can die flowing, becoming one with the flowing water, a peaceful flow into another life."

As I experienced my dream by becoming the parts of it, I found myself relaxing and feeling peaceful again. My panic disappeared. I felt the flow of life surge through me. I could flow tenderly with Eta and become one with her, and with the world we shared.

The lessons from this dream were many for me and most are apparent. But the one which looms up for me concerns flowing with my environment—flowing with others rather than battling or manipulating them. My discovery that the water held the answer with its flow was an important experience for me, and it revealed a difference between knowledge and wisdom. The fact that its flow might lead me to an escape route was important knowledge. But the discovery that it could also help me flow into another life and become one with the world was wisdom. Wisdom must be discovered. It cannot be taught. The stream contained wisdom as did the eternal river flowing through life in Hesse's great novel, *Siddhartha*.

The river has taught me to listen; you will learn from it too. The river knows everything, one can learn everything from it. . . . Above all, he learned from it how to listen, to listen with a still heart, with a waiting, open soul. . . .The river is everywhere at the same time, at the source

and at the mouth, at the waterfall, at the ferry, at the current, in the
ocean and in the mountains, everywhere, and the present only exists
for it, not the shadow of the past, nor the shadow of the future. . . . I
reviewed my life and it was also a river.*

*Hermann Hesse, *Siddhartha* (New York: New Directions, 1951), pp. 86–
87.

Epilogue:
The Rivers of Our Lives,
the Bridges of Our Sharing

My life is a series of unfoldings and awakenings, and as I grow through one I find that it takes some time to assimilate it before I move on. It's as though I am cascading down a waterfall into the placid pool that lies below. Then I think, "Look where I am!" I bask in the peacefulness for a while, and then slowly I find myself being drawn toward some new place. I know I have farther to go on my journey. The current picks me up, and I am tugged toward the next fall until I am drawn over the awesome precipice and cascade down to the next still pool, with new awareness and wisdom. The process keeps repeating. My life keeps moving.

At times I feel that I am even growing in courage to accept death by strengthening my own selfhood, by surrendering to superhuman destinies. Surrender appears again as an ally. When I am centered in myself, I can acknowledge the conflicting forces within me by surrendering to my own confusion, letting them be there, and letting a natural movement forward arise from within these tensions.

Of all the fears with which men live, perhaps our fear of death is the strongest. A man who has been able to ennoble his fear—fear of death, fear of failure, fear of the unknown—by transforming part of it into awe of life's rhythms has grown. I have discovered that part of my fear really is awe. It helps to transform my fear into an acceptance and an awe both of my own powers and of these powers within me which are not "mine." I am not sure when my present drama will end or the next awakening begin, with a plunge over the next waterfall, or down the river of life.

I want my next stage of growing to contain much more leisure and time for reflection and personal relationships, for pursuing things in depth, for reading and writing, as well as time for spiritual growth. My fantasy (and many do come true) is that my growing will never end until I reach the last cascade in my life and take the frightening plunge over this final water-fall into the stream of my next life.

I have had visions of returning—of being reincarnated—as one of my son Eric's sons. I dreamed such a dream one night, and who am I now to deny that it may come true? I am open to believing that my spirit may return in another life.

In many ways my present stage has held its share of painful difficulties. From many of them I feel I have learned. Others have just happened.

Where will my river of life lead? I can already hear the frightening thunder of the next waterfall, and I know I must flow to it. I also know that the river forks in many more places. Some of the forks lead to tranquil and still pools—which often become stagnant. Others are cascading down the mountain of my universe with frightening speed, slowing down only momentarily from pool to pool; the risks are high in shooting such rapids. Which fork of the river should I take? Perhaps I'll flow with the natural currents of life at the next fork, rather than programming my route ahead, as I have struggled to do so often in my life.

Finally, something is apparent to me that I am discovering is present in many lives: a snarl of contradiction and confusion. I am finding that we have so many interesting polarities that we often feel confused. Life may be simple, as Lawrence Durrell suggests, but we human beings certainly are not. Often we experience our multiple abilities and awareness as a source of worry rather than wonder. Why?

I have found that, to the degree I "program" my way out of my confusion, or force myself to clear it up, or deny it, I wind up avoiding my real feelings and deceiving myself. Then I end up more confused than ever. My life is a contradiction: from West Point to Esalen; a frightened boy and successful executive; tender and strong; tough and weak; love and hate; satisfaction and despair; heart and head; sinner and innocent. I am only now beginning to accept and surrender to the experience of being all these things. The place where my polarities meet, somewhere within me, is my impasse. This is the place where I am stuck and where my pain exists. Yet it is also where, after I surrender to myself, my joy begins to flow and my aliveness grows. My impasse is so close to my source. Let go. Let go. Don't push the flowing currents.

The river of my life is my own personal solitude and quest. In these pages—which reflect no approved solutions for anyone, not even for me—some of my struggles are laid open and my pain made visible. For me, a person from a closed, restricted, tough way of life, just the process of opening to you is a freeing experience. I appreciate your making a space in your life for me to share this part of mine.

My wish for all of us is that, by throwing this rope bridge of words out across the chasms of my—of our—solitude, we can reach out and find one another a little more easily as we travel along the paths of our own journeys. It is an adventure well worth sharing.

Index

About the Author

Harold C. Lyon, Jr., has had an unusual background, having served in top echelons of government as Assistant Deputy U.S. Commissioner of Education, Deputy Associate Commissioner, and Federal Director of Education for the Gifted and Talented. In the academic world, he has served as Assistant to the President of Ohio University; he has taught at the University of Massachusetts, Georgetown University (in Psychology), and Antioch College, where he is currently Abraham Maslow Professor. He has a doctorate from the University of Massachusetts and is a licensed psychologist and therapist. Dr. Lyon has been a leader in the human potential movement for some years. He is the author of a best-selling textbook, *Learning to Feel—Feeling to Learn* (Charles Merrill, 1971), and a book, *It's Me and I'm Here!* (Delacorte, 1974), highlighting some of his own personal growth experiences from West Point (from which he graduated and later served seven years as a Ranger-paratrooper Army officer), to Esalen. Dr. Lyon, who has two children and five step-children, is a member of MENSA, the National Advisory

Board of est, and a founding trustee of American Excellence.

In addition to his teaching, writing, and practice as a therapist, he is presently developing plans for a non-athletic "Olympics" for gifted youth of the world.